About the Au

Ian Parmenter was born in post-war London and survived nine years of British cooking before his parents moved to Belgium and, to his great relief, took him with them. In Brussels, the city famous for its sprouts, he began his love affair with food. The Belgian national dish of chips with mayonnaise was the first he learnt to master. His adventures with continental cuisine were curtailed when he was sent back to England to further his education at an ancient British school, where he was forced to eat ancient British food, such as hot tinned pilchards on toast. He had to develop his cooking skills secretly in the chemistry lab with a bunsen burner. He claims his fish finger and baked bean casserole cooked in a conical flask is still remembered with great affection by the year of '64.

On graduation, Ian began a career in journalism which took him to Fleet Street's better eating and drinking establishments, where he remained for 7 years long enough to acquire the itch.

His palate jaded by years of smoked mackerel pate and ploughman's lunches, Ian fled to Australia arriving in the early seventies, a period not known for its sophisticated food culture. He remembers one of his first hotel breakfasts being lamb chops, fried eggs, bacon, beetroot and cold lumpy gravy washed down with weak black instant coffee with a slice of orange rind in it.

Joining the ABC in 1973, Ian soon moved into television production. In 1995 he won the *Prix de la Profession* at the first *World Festival of Television Gastronomy* in Deauville, France.

CONSUMING *Passions*
with
Ian Parmenter

Killeen

Published and distributed
exclusively in the European Union by
Killeen Books,
Killeen,
Blackrock Village,
Cork City,
Ireland.

First published in Australia
This revised edition is published by Killeen Books in 1996
1 3 5 6 4 2

ISBN 1-873548-41-9

Set in Adobe Garamond by the publishers.
Colour separations prepared by Upper Case Ltd.

Printed by the Guernsey Press.

Contents

Soups & Stocks

Entrees & Nibbles

Vegetables and Salads

Stuffed Artichokes 42
Leek and Ham Gratin 43

Fish and Seafood

Moroccan Fish 46
Pickled Sardines with Aioli 47
Ginger Fish Sauna 48
Fish Cakes with Cucumber Relish 50
Fish and Vegetable Stir-fry 51
Orange Prawns with Noodles 53
Ravioli of Lobster with Tomato and Basil sauce 54

Poultry

Chicken Pecan Terrine 57
Onion and Citrus Chutney 58
Chicken Waterzooi 59
Chicken with Tangy Plum Sauce 61
Hunter Chicken 62
Grape Chicken Idea 63
Chicken and Leek Pancakes 65
Chicken Prawn Fandango 67
Chicken Chardonnay 68
Lemon Chicken 69

Meats

Pork And Orange Roll 72
Orange Glazed Christmas Ham 73
Pork and Apple Pie 74
Apple and Orange Sauce 76
Herbed Lamb Balls 77
Apricot and Herb 78
Stuffed Loin of Pork 78
Lamb Kebabs with Tabbouleh 79
Hazelnut Cream Dressing 80

Eggs

Fruit Desserts

Soups & Stocks

Pistou Resistance

The French call this a soup. They are being unduly modest. Pistou is a supercharged gastronomic scene stealer. It is a triumph not just because it is a great vegetable soup, but because it's served with a mixture which gives it its name, a delicious sauce of basil, garlic and olive oil. It is within reach of those of us who are able to acquire fresh basil . For the rest of you — I'm deeply sorry. If you plan to serve it as an entrée, you'll only need a very light main course, perhaps a grilled sardine on a lettuce leaf. **Heart Foundation Approved.**

Serves 8

INGREDIENTS
THE SOUP
2 large onions, sliced into rings
2 leeks, sliced into rings
2 sticks celery, diced
2 large potatoes, cubed
2 carrots, sliced
200 g fresh green beans, chopped into bite size pieces
200 g dried beans (haricot, kidney etc.)
5 or 6 cloves garlic crushed
2 Tbsp extra virgin olive oil
200 g cooked macaroni
2 litres water (approx.)

The Pistou Sauce
3 cloves garlic, finely chopped
1 cup chopped fresh basil

Method

The day before, soak the dried beans in cold water. Using a heavy saucepan or stockpot, gently cook the onions, leeks, carrots and celery for 5 minutes in the olive oil. Add soaked dried beans, green beans, potato pieces and garlic. Cover with water and simmer for 1½ hours. Just before serving, season to taste and stir in the macaroni.

To make sauce: Pound the fresh basil and garlic in a mortar — or blender. Add egg yolk. Gradually stir in the olive oil, starting a few drops at a time — as you would a mayonnaise. The mixture should thicken.

To serve: Put a small dollop of sauce in each warmed bowl and a sprinkle of Parmesan cheese. Then pour on a good amount of soup and ask everyone to wait a full 2 minutes, savouring the wonderful aroma, before stirring the mixture up well and eating with tremendous enthusiasm. Truly, this is one of the world's great dishes.

Note: The pistou sauce will go brown if exposed for a long time to air. It sort of rusts. This is not a problem, except that it can look unsightly. The solutions are either to put it in an airtight jar and cover with a thin layer of olive oil or to make up the sauce immediately before serving. The sauce will keep in the refrigerator for several days.

Bacon Hock and Lentil Soup

The lentil is one of nature's smallest vitamin pills. It contains B-group vitamins, thiamin, niacin and B6. It's also supercharged with minerals, potassium, magnesium and zinc. Here, it is teamed with bacon hocks or shanks to make a robust and nourishing soup. If the bacon has been salt cured and/or smoked, soak it in water overnight before using. **Heart Foundation approved.**

Serves 6

INGREDIENTS
2 medium carrots, finely diced
1 leek, washed and finely cut
1 celeriac, peeled and finely diced or
1 cup chopped celery
4 or 5 cloves garlic, crushed
2½ Tbsp oil (preferably a strongly flavoured olive oil)
200g red lentils, well washed and drained
½ tsp grated nutmeg
½ tsp ground fennel seed
6 Tbsp finely chopped parsley
3 Tbsp finely chopped mint
1 bacon hock, all fat removed
1 litre chicken, veal or vegetable stock
60g grated parmesan cheese
Pepper to taste

METHOD
In a stock pot or large saucepan gently cook the carrots, leek, celeriac or celery and garlic in 1 Tbsp oil for 3-4 minutes. Add drained lentils and stir while continuing to cook for about 30 seconds. Stir in nutmeg and fennel. Stir in about 2 Tbsp of the parsley and 1 Tbsp of the mint. Reserve the remainder for the pesto sauce. Add the bacon hock and stock, put on the lid and simmer

soup very slowly for at least 1½ hours. Meanwhile, make up a pesto sauce by pounding in a mortar (or blending) the remaining parsley and mint with the parmesan cheese and 1½ Tbsp oil until a smooth paste is achieved. Season with pepper. When hock is cooked, remove and cut meat into bite-sized pieces. To serve: Put bacon pieces into individual soup bowls, pour over soup and top with a spoonful of the pesto sauce.

Serving suggestion: Accompany with crusty bread.
Leftover potential: Keeps well for several days in the refrigerator.

Spicy Potato and Pumpkin Soup

Two of our most popular and least expensive vegetables team up to make a fabulous dish with a hint of the Orient. **Heart Foundation approved**.

Serves 6

INGREDIENTS
1 kg potatoes, peeled
1 medium sized butternut pumpkin
1 litre chicken or vegetable stock
2 Tbsp chopped spring onions
1 Tbsp oil (olive, canola or peanut)
2 tsp finely chopped or minced ginger
2 or 3 cloves garlic, finely chopped or minced
1 tsp ground coriander
1 Tbsp fresh coriander leaves, finely chopped
Juice of 1 orange and a few strips of rind
2 Tbsp coconut cream
2 tsp chilli sauce (optional)
Pepper to taste

Few strips red sweet pepper for garnish (optional)

METHOD

Cut potatoes into 2 cm cubes. Peel pumpkin and cut into 2 cm cubes. Put potato and pumpkin pieces into a stock pot or large saucepan. Add stock. If vegetables are not completely covered, add water until they are. Simmer gently, uncovered, until the vegetables are just cooked they should not disintegrate in the pot. Meanwhile, in a separate saucepan, Sauté most of the spring onions in the oil for 2-3 minutes. Reserve some of the spring onions for garnish. Add ginger, garlic and coriander and cook gently for about 1 minute longer. Add orange juice and orange rind (it will be removed later) and reduce by cooking uncovered for 5-6 minutes. Reserve a few pieces of potato and pumpkin for garnish, then press the rest through a fine strainer or blend in a food processor to make a purée. Add the puréed potato and pumpkin to the other pan and simmer slowly for 5 minutes. Remove soup from heat and add coconut cream and chilli sauce (if using). Season with pepper. Once the coconut cream has been added to the soup it should not boil again. *To serve*: Ladle soup into warm bowls and garnish with reserved potato and pumpkin, finely grated orange rind, remaining spring onions and red sweet pepper (if using). *Leftover potential*: Is fine warmed through or served cold.

Spinach and Chick Pea Soup

A thoroughly healthy and nourishing soup with just a hint of spice.
Heart Foundation approved.

Serves 4

INGREDIENTS
200g chick peas, soaked in water overnight
2 onion quarters
2 or 3 cloves
2 bay leaves
1 head of garlic (yes, that's a lot of cloves of garlic!), loose dry outer
skin removed
500g fresh spinach
1 tsp sesame oil
1 Tbsp extra virgin olive oil
2 cloves garlic finely chopped
2 Tbsp freshly made breadcrumbs
3 Tbsp chopped parsley
2 Tbsp chopped coriander leaves and/or
½ tsp ground coriander
1 tsp chilli sauce (optional)
To serve cold
1 Tbsp finely diced tomato flesh
1 Tbsp finely diced sweet pepper
1 Tbsp finely diced Lebanese cucumber

METHOD
Drain chick peas. Put in a large saucepan and cover with water.
Stud onion quarters with cloves. Add onion, bay leaves and the
whole head of garlic to the pan. Simmer very slowly for 1 hour or
so until the chick peas are cooked — they should still be firm, but
not crunchy. Meanwhile, strip the spinach leaves from the stalks.
Wash and drain, but not too thoroughly — some water may

remain on the leaves. In a large saucepan, gently cook spinach leaves in the sesame oil for about 1 minute or until they wilt. Remove spinach from pan. Add the olive oil, finely chopped garlic, breadcrumbs and parsley to the pan and cook for 2-3 minutes. Crush garlic/bread mixture to a pulp with 2-3 tspn of the cooking water from the chick peas. Set aside. When the chick peas are cooked, remove the head of garlic and onion segments. Squeeze garlic paste from the cooked garlic. Add garlic paste, spinach and bread mixture to chick peas and cooking water. Add coriander and season to taste before serving. Reheat if serving hot. *To serve cold*: Chill soup. Serve garnished soup with diced tomato, sweet pepper and cucumber.

Leftover potential: The soup keeps for two or three days in the refrigerator.

Taking Stock

Stock is one of the important components of thousands of savoury dishes, and stock-making is one of the first techniques taught to food professionals. European restaurateurs hold their stock pots in such high esteem that some boast that they are still constantly adding to a batch of stock which was started more than a hundred years ago and has never been taken off the fire. If I'm always stressing the importance of homemade stock, it's for two good reasons. Firstly, a well-made stock will help many a culinary endeavour to become a triumph. Secondly, making your own stock means you can keep to a minimum the amount of fat and salt it contains. Remember, stock powders and cubes are very high in sodium. True, it does take work and time to prepare stock, but once made it can be stored conveniently in the freezer.

Once you get into the habit of making your own stock you will never look back. And if you build up a rapport with your butcher and fishmonger, they will probably not charge you for the bones which are used to from the basis.

Essentially, there are four types of stock: meat, chicken, fish and vegetable, and the technique for making them is similar. Ingredients are immersed in water, simmered to allow the flavours to infuse the liquor, strained, skimmed of fat, reduced and clarified if necessary. The following stock ideas represent a basis from which to work. I recommend you try these and adapt them to suit your own taste. There are countless variations on a theme given the wide range of meats, poultry, fish, seafood, vegetables, herbs and spices available.

Meat stock

There are two ways of making meat stock; a white stock can be made using bones as they come from the butcher; the other has them browned in the oven before boiling them up to give a darker stock, which could be further coloured with the addition of tomatoes or tomato paste. Veal or beef leg bones make good stock, as do the bone of game. Get the butcher to crack the bones for you to release the most flavour.

Some of the cheaper cuts of meat have terrific flavour and can be included in the stock pot. Put the bones and meat in a stock pot or large saucepan and cover with water. Allow the water to cover the ingredients by a few centimetres. Bring the water to boiling point, turn down the heat and simmer the mixture for 10 minutes before skimming off the particles which have floated to the surface. Stir in about 1 cup of cold water and simmer for a further 15 minutes. Repeat the process of skimming off the surface scum. Add finely chopped onion, carrot, leek, celery, garlic cloves, a few peppercorns and a *bouquet garni* — made up of a couple of sprigs of thyme, a handful of parsley and a couple of bay leaves. Also add tomatoes if desired. Continue to simmer for at least 6 hours, or overnight.

Strain and reduce the stock by two-thirds, adding tomato purée at this stage, if using. Remove fat by pouring most of it off. Remove the rest by laying a sheet of paper towel on the surface of the stock, then carefully remove the paper towel, taking with it the surface fat. Repeat the process until all you see on the surface are a few small, fatty globules. Or, refrigerate and lift off the fat when it has solidified. Store in ice-cube trays in the freezer. Wrap the trays in plastic food wrap when the stock has frozen.

Chicken Stock

Place chicken bones and necks in a stock pot or large saucepan and cover with water. Allow water to cover the bones by three or four centimetres. Bring the water to boiling point, then turn down the heat and allow the mixture to simmer for 10 minutes before skimming off the particles which have floated to the surface. Add finely chopped onion, carrot, leek, celery, garlic cloves, a few peppercorns and a *bouquet garni* — made by tying together a couple of sprigs of thyme, a handful of parsley and a couple of bay leaves. I wouldn't substitute the fresh herbs with dried ones. Continue to simmer for a couple of hours. Don't overcook the bones or the stock will become bitter. Strain and reduce the stock by two-thirds. Remove fat from the stock by pouring off most of it. Remove the rest by laying a sheet of paper towel on the surface of the stock, then carefully remove the paper towel. When you remove the paper towel the surface fat will be taken with it. Repeat the process until all you see on the surface are a few small fatty globules. Or, refrigerate and lift off the fat when it has solidified. Store in ice cube trays In the freezer. Wrap the trays in plastic wrap when the stock has frozen.

Fish Stock

I rarely make this stock, except in winter and with the exhaust fans working at full capacity. At other times of year the aromas can become too overpowering, especially if conditions are still and humid. I use fish bones, heads and tails of gently flavoured fish such as snapper, flounder, dhufish and whiting, avoiding the more oily fish such as mackerel. I also add prawn and lobster heads and shells.

Everything is simply put in a stock pot or large saucepan with a handful of parsley, a finely sliced onion, a couple of bay leaves and a finely sliced leek and covered with water. The mixture is then simmered over very low heat for 15-20 minutes. The water should be just boiling. If the stock is too long on the heat it will become bitter. Strain and reduce the stock by two-thirds.

Store in ice cube trays in the freezer. Wrap the trays in plastic wrap when the stock has frozen otherwise the stock may attract odours from other foods in the freezer.

Vegetable Stock

There are cooks who use the stock pot as a dumping ground for their kitchen off-cuts. I like to use the basic combination of onion, leek, carrot, celery, garlic, thyme, parsley, a bay leaf and a few peppercorns, and begin the process by browning the vegetables in a little olive oil before adding water. The ingredients are simmered for an hour or so before the stock is strained and reduced to a third of its volume.

Salt

I never add salt to a stock. There are salts naturally occurring in most stocks, and since the stock is an adjunct to other components of a dish, I season later.

Clarifying Stock

The way egg white clarifies stock is one of the great culinary wonders of the world. Once the stock has been strained, reduced, and allowed to cool, stir in a couple of lightly beaten egg whites. Stirring gently once or twice, slowly heat the stock. As it reaches boiling point the egg white will firm, along with any particles which have clouded the stock. Strain the stock through a piece of muslin or a clean cotton cloth. You will finish with a beautiful clear liquid — loaded with Bliss factor!

Aspic

When a good, concentrated, clear meat or fish stock cools it will form a jelly made from the collagen which has been released from the bones. This may be used as a coating or garnish with cold meat or fish dishes. To thicken further, gelatine may be used according to manufacturers instructions.

Entrees & Nibbles

Olive Focaccia

Along with the olive and wine, bread and other wheat products have been the basis of the Mediterranean diet for centuries. This olive bread is a joy to make and works as well with dried yeast as it does with the fresh variety. **Heart Foundation approved.**

Makes 2 loaves

INGREDIENTS
250g plain white flour
1 tsp sugar
1 x 7g sachet dried yeast
1½ cups tepid water
250g wholemeal flour
2 Tbsp olive oil
1 medium onion, finely chopped
2 Tbsp olives, stoned and chopped (preferably black)
2 Tbsp fresh herbs of choice (preferably rosemary, parsley, oregano and thyme) or 1 tsp mixed dried herbs
Additional plain flour for kneading
Additional olives for final stage (these may be left unstoned)

METHOD
Mix together 1 Tbsp white flour, the sugar, yeast and 2 Tbsp of the tepid water and stand for 20 minutes. This activates the yeast and the mixture should be frothy. Mix the remaining white flour, the wholemeal flour and 1 Tbsp olive oil in a bowl. Add yeast mixture and remaining water and mix well. Cover with a damp tea towel and leave in a warm place for 1 hour. Meanwhile, heat the

remaining oil in a frying pan and cook onion over medium heat for 5 minutes, or until it softens. Stir in chopped olives and herbs and cook for about 30 seconds, then set aside. Knead dough on a floured work surface for 5-6 minutes. Knead in olive/onion/herb mixture. (It doesn't matter if bits of olive fall out, just poke them back in). Divide dough into two portions. Flatten each piece of dough into a fat pizza shape and put on an oiled pizza or baking tray. Cover with a damp tea towel and leave in a warm place for an hour or until risen. Before baking, dimple surface of each loaf with your fingers, drizzle with a little more olive oil and scatter with additional olives. (Sprinkle with a little sea salt, if you like). Bake at 200°C for about 25 minutes, or until top is golden brown and bottom is light brown.

Leftover potential: Does not keep well beyond a day. *Hint*: Although there are those who believe the contrary, dough will rise perfectly well without salt, and the olives may well be salty enough, so you may wish to leave seasoning until after the bread is cooked.

Twice-cooked Kervella Goat Cheese Soufflés

I acquired this recipe from Gary Jones, an exceptionally talented chef whose Perth restaurant, San Lorenzo, won the prestigious *Remy Gourmet* Restaurant of the Year Award in 1995. He now has a new restaurant, Jones, in Melbourne. This dish makes a great entrée which, because, of it's richness, should be followed by a light main course. Gary uses Gabrielle Kervella's goat cheese from Western Australia, but you could substitute with other goat cheese.

Serves 10 as an entrée

INGREDIENTS
½ cup freshly grated parmesan cheese plus 2 Tbsp extra
1 litre full cream milk
medium onion
1 bay leaf
3 cloves
200g unsalted butter
200g plain flour
240g goat cheese, roughly chopped
10 egg yolks
½ tsp ground nutmeg
½ tsp cayenne pepper
Salt and pepper to taste
12 egg whites
500ml whipping cream

METHOD
Grease ten 1-cup capacity ramekins or cups with butter. Sprinkle with some of the parmesan cheese to coat. Heat the milk in a large saucepan until almost boiling. Remove from heat, add onion, bay leaf and cloves and stand to infuse for 10 minutes.

Melt butter in a separate saucepan, stir in flour and cook over medium heat for 1 minute. Strain milk and slowly pour into the butter/flour mixture. Cook, stirring frequently, until a thick sauce forms. Add the goat cheese and ½ cup of parmesan cheese. When cheese has melted, whisk in egg yolks and beat well. Add nutmeg, cayenne pepper and a pinch of salt and pepper Whisk egg whites until stiff peaks form, then fold into cheese mixture. Divide mixture between prepared ramekins. Place on baking trays and bake at 170°C for 20 minutes. Remove from oven and set aside for 30 minutes. Turn soufflés out into ovenproof dishes, sprinkle with remaining parmesan cheese and pour over cream. Bake at 180°C for 10 minutes, then brown under a preheated grill until golden.

Leftover potential: Poor.

Fondues Bruxelloises

These fondues bear no relation to what we normally think of as fondues. Rather, they are deep-fried cheese squares, which could have been the inspiration behind deep-frying camembert cheese. This is a much more cost effective way of deep-frying cheese and is a very popular Belgian entrée.

Serves 12 as an appetiser

INGREDIENTS
100g butter
150g plain flour
500ml milk
150g Swiss cheese (Emmental or Gruyere), grated
100g Parmesan cheese, grated
¼ tsp cayenne pepper
½ tsp grated nutmeg
6 egg yolks
Salt and white pepper to taste
3 eggs
2 tsp water
1 Tbsp oil
Flour for dusting
Breadcrumbs
Oil for deep-frying

METHOD
The day before, or the morning of the day of serving…melt butter in heavy based saucepan. Stir in flour. When mixed, gradually stir in milk. Bring to boiling point and cook, stirring constantly, over low heat for 2 minutes. Remove pan from heat, stir in cheeses and mix until melted. Return to heat, add cayenne pepper, nutmeg, the

6 egg yolks and salt and pepper. Simmer, stirring constantly, for 3 minutes. Do not allow the mixture to boil. Pour mixture into a greased or oiled 23 x 32cm baking tin lined with baking paper. Spread mixture evenly over base of tin, then cover with a sheet of baking paper and set aside to cool. When cool, put in the refrigerator. You could speed the process by putting the mixture in the freezer but don't allow it to freeze solid. The next day (or later in the day)…beat the 3 eggs until frothy, mix in water, oil and a little salt and pepper. Turn cheese mixture out and roll into sausage shapes about the size of large fish fingers. Dust each sausage with flour, then dip into egg mixture and shake off excess. Roll in breadcrumbs and again shake off excess. Deep-fry until golden and drain on paper towels.

Serving suggestion: Serve on shredded lettuce leaves (preferably not iceberg).
Leftover potential: Poor.
Hint: Once egged and breadcrumbed, the fondues will keep well in the freezer. I like to serve half as an appetiser for a dinner of six and reserve the rest for another occasion.

Hot Tamales with Chilli Tomato Salsa

This is a classic from South of the border, down Mexico way. Small savoury parcels are steamed and served hot with a cool salsa of fresh tomatoes, herbs, lemon and olive oil. They should be served chilli hot, but are also tasty served mild. The amounts of chilli I have included here make medium-hot tamales. The masa harina flour should be available in larger supermarkets, delicatessens and health food stores.

Makes 20

INGREDIENTS
1 sweet corn cob
2 cups masa harina flour
1 cup good oil (such as olive, walnut or macadamia)
500ml chicken stock
100g chopped cooked chicken
50g chopped black olives
½ medium onion, finely chopped
2 tsp minced chilli

For Salsa
500g peeled, seeded and finely diced tomatoes
2 cloves garlic, finely chopped
1 Tbsp chopped oregano leaves (or 1 tsp dried oregano)
1 Tbsp chopped basil leaves
2 Tbsp lemon juice
2 tsp minced chilli
2 Tbsp olive oil
Pepper to taste

METHOD
Cut 20 squares of non-stick baking paper each measuring approximately 15cm. Cut corn kernels away from the cob. Break into individual kernels and brown in a dry saucepan over medium heat for about 5 minutes. Mix together masa harina flour and oil. Add chicken stock, a little at a time. Mix constantly, until a smooth, but firm, dough is formed. Mix together corn, chicken, olives, onion and chilli and gently fold into the dough. Roll about a dessertspoon of dough into a small sausage shape and place on a square of the baking paper. Wrap up to make a parcel. Repeat to

use all papers and/or dough. Place parcels in a bamboo, or other, steamer and steam for 30 minutes. To make salsa: Mix together all salsa ingredients.

Leftover potential: Best eaten the day they're made.

Mushroom Rice Magic

One of my favourite savoury dishes is mushroom risotto It tastes superb, but one of the problems is that an old style mushroom risotto can often acquire a deathly grey look, which makes the whole experience a turn off unless you sit in the dark to eat it! Not so with this *Consuming Passions* recipe which uses pre-cooked long grain rice. **Heart Foundation approved.**

Serves 4

INGREDIENTS
2 Tbsp chopped spring onions, white part only
1 Tbsp extra virgin olive oil
1 cup pre-cooked long grain rice
250g mushrooms, cut into small pieces, stalks included
1 Tbsp finely chopped parsley
½ tsp ground mace or nutmeg
500ml chicken stock (or vegetable stock)
1 Tbsp grated parmesan cheese
2 Tbsp chopped spring onions, green part only, for garnish

METHOD

Sauté white parts of spring onions in 1 tspn olive oil over medium heat for 2-3 minutes to soften. Stir in rice and cook for 2 minutes, or until golden.

Meanwhile, in a separate frying pan, sauté mushrooms in remaining oil for 2-3 minutes. If they stick, add a little water, a teaspoon at a time — they must not stew! Stir in parsley and mace or nutmeg, then remove from heat and set aside. Stir stock into rice, reduce heat, cover pan and simmer very slowly for 20 minutes. Check to see if rice is cooked — the grains should be tender and separate. If the rice mixture seems too dry, add a little water (a couple of tablespoons) and stand for 5 minutes. Stir mushrooms and parmesan cheese into rice.

Garnish with green parts of spring onions and serve.

Leftover potential: I enjoy it cold or reheated.

Broccoli Pasta

A quick vegetarian pasta dish that I discovered on a visit to Rome. **Heart Foundation approved.**

Serves 4

INGREDIENTS
1 head broccoli cut into florets
2 cloves garlic, finely chopped
1 Tbsp olive oil
½ tspn saffron strands
1 Tbsp hot vegetable stock
2 Tbsp pine nuts, lightly toasted
2 Tbsp raisins
1 red chilli, seeded and finely sliced
1 Tbsp fresh breadcrumbs

2 tsp olive oil
500g cooked fusilli pasta

METHOD
Steam or boil broccoli for 4-5 minutes, or until just cooked. Plunge
into iced water to set colour, then drain. Cook garlic in the 1 Tbsp
olive oil. Pound garlic and oil to make a pulp. Steep saffron strands
in hot stock. Crush broccoli with a fork or potato masher. Place in
a frying pan, then add pine nuts, raisins, chilli and garlic pulp and
warm through. Stir in saffron mixture. Brown breadcrumbs in 2
tsp olive oil. Spoon broccoli mixture over fusilli and sprinkle with
browned breadcrumbs.
Hint: Serve this dish immediately after it is cooked. If kept too long
before serving, the broccoli will oxidise, look yellow and not taste
wonderful.

Ricotta and Spinach Cannelloni

Pasta is a fabulous food, coming as it does in all shapes, colours and
sizes. Made with either wheat or semolina, it is high in energy
derived from the carbohydrate, and is non-fattening. That is, until
you start adding things to it. This recipe uses two light but tasty
sauces with cannelloni. The tubular pasta is filled with a ricotta and
spinach stuffing, then simmered in tomato sauce before being
topped with a light bechamel.
Heart Foundation approved.

Serves 4

INGREDIENTS
½ medium onion finely chopped
3 cloves garlic, peeled and crushed

2 Tbsp extra virgin olive oil
300ml tomato pulp or purée (not the concentrated paste)
½ tsp sugar
1 bunch spinach or 100 g cooked spinach
250g ricotta cheese
25g parmesan cheese
¼ tsp ground mace or nutmeg
White pepper to taste
20g polyunsaturated margarine
30g cornflour
300ml reduced fat milk
1 cup chopped parsley
12 cannelloni tubes (the kind that doesn't need pre-cooking)

METHOD

Sauté onion and garlic in 1 Tbsp olive oil until softened.
Stir in tomato pulp or purée and sugar. Remove from heat. Pour into a baking dish and spread evenly over base. Wash spinach and drain. Remove stalks and chop leaves. In the pan in which the sauce was cooked (it is unnecessary to wash the pan), put remaining oil and cook spinach for 2 minutes. Transfer spinach to a mixing bowl and cool slightly. Stir in ricotta cheese, parmesan cheese, mace or nutmeg and white pepper. Transfer mixture to a bowl to cool. In the same pan (again, washing is unnecessary), melt the margarine. Add cornflour and cook, stirring, for 1 minute over low heat. Slowly add milk and cook, stirring constantly, until sauce thickens. Add chopped parsley and season to taste. With spoon or piping bag, fill the cannelloni tubes with the spinach and cheese mixture. Place the filled tubes on the tomato sauce in the baking dish. Cover cannelloni with the parsley bechamel sauce and sprinkle with additional parmesan cheese, if you wish. Cover with foil and bake at 180°C for at least 25 minutes, remove foil and bake for 20 minutes longer to allow the top to brown.

꙳

Leftover potential: Good. May be reheated or refreshed by adding more sauce topping.

Ego Noodles

No, it's not a misprint. Ego noodles is a simple dish of pasta that is so rewarding to prepare that it's good for any cook's ego. It relies for its success on silverbeet, or as it's otherwise known, seakale, Swiss chard or *Beta vulgaris*. **Heart Foundation approved**
Serves 4

INGREDIENTS
375g packet egg noodles
1 bunch silverbeet
1 medium onion, chopped
2 cloves garlic, crushed
250g ricotta
1 Tbsp olive oil
1 tspn chilli sauce or sprinkling chilli powder
½ tspn grated nutmeg
Black pepper to taste
1 tspn fresh ginger, chopped (optional)
50g parmesan cheese, grated

METHOD
Cook pasta in lots of boiling water until aldente. Drain. Strip green leaves from the silverbeet stalks. Wash well and drain. Chop into 2cm strips. Leave on towel to dry. (The stalks may be used in other dishes.) In large frying pan or wok, gently cook onion, garlic and ginger for 5 minutes. Increase heat. Add chilli sauce and nutmeg.

Stir well. Stir in silverbeet strips. Cook over high heat while stirring all the time until silverbeet has softened but still has some bite left in it. Reduce heat. Mix in noodles and crumble in ricotta. Toss in parmesan cheese and mix well. Season with black pepper and serve.

Mushroom Tagliatelle

What makes this dish particularly appealing is the handful of chopped parsley thrown over it before serving. A flat-leafed variety known as Italia parsley is preferable for this dish as it is more flavoursome than the common curly-leafed variety.

Serves 4 to 6

INGREDIENTS
500g sliced mushrooms
500g fresh or dried tagliatelle
2 Tbsp olive oil
1 garlic clove, crushed
1 small glass of white wine
½ cup chopped parsley
Pepper to taste

METHOD
Cook the pasta in a large saucepan of boiling water until al dente. Drain. Make the sauce by heating the oil in a frying pan. Add chopped mushrooms and cook for 2 or 3 minutes. Add wine and garlic. Simmer gently until the wine has almost evaporated. Toss the cooked pasta with the mushrooms and parsley. Season with black pepper. Serve with a large, fresh, crispy, green salad and fresh crusty Italian loaf. An Australian chardonnay provides excellent accompaniment.

Vegetables and Salads

There is an old saying that the English have three vegetables, two of which are cabbage. And when I grew up in England that seemed almost to be the case. I remember potatoes, peas, carrots, cabbage and not much else. Most of it was boiled to a pulp

Nowadays, the range of vegetables available to most of us is fantastic. As a result of refrigerated transport, however, most varieties are available all year round, which means that we are buying expensive overseas produce out of season, rather than waiting to eat locally grown vegetables when they are at their best. And cheapest.

As well as being beautiful to eat, vegetables generally are low in fat, high in fibre and rich in vitamins.

When buying vegetables, look for the local-grown. The colour should be bright and the vegetable firm. Avoid those which show evidence of old age wilted leaves and discoloration and those which are gigantic, their growth was probably forced and they may be tasteless.

Root vegetables are best stored at cool temperatures, ideally not more than 15°C. Soft, leafy vegetables, such as lettuces, should be stored loosely wrapped in the crisper compartment of the refrigerator. Store vegetables away from fruit and do not wash them until just before you prepare them for cooking or eating. Moisture can hasten the rotting process and may leach out vitamins.

Much of a vegetable's flavour and goodness may be near the surface so it's a good idea where possible to eat the skin.

Certain vegetables contain bitter juices which should be removed before cooking. Most notable is the aubergine, which should be sliced, sprinkled with salt and left to stand for at least 30 minutes. Then rinse well to remove the salt and bitterness, and dry with paper towel before cooking.

Other vegetables, which are no longer as young as they would like to be, might also need to go through this process: courgette and cucumbers, for instance.

Some vegetables benefit from blanching which removes any very strong flavours. This process of plunging them into boiling water for a few moments also prevents discolouring. After blanching, vegetables may be kept overnight in the refrigerator.

Spicy Italian-Style Cauliflower

This makes a change to plain, steamed cauliflower. It takes only a few more minutes to prepare and goes superbly with most meat dishes. **Heart Foundation approved.**

Serves 4 to 6

INGREDIENTS
1 whole cauliflower, broken into florets
1 Tbsp virgin olive oil
3 garlic cloves, minced
1 tspn chilli sauce
2 Tbsp white wine
Freshly ground pepper

METHOD

Steam the cauliflower for 10 minutes or until tender but still firm. Drain. Heat the olive oil over medium heat in a non-stick pan and sauté the garlic for 1 minute. Add the chilli sauce, then the cauliflower and wine. Sauté, stirring for 3 to 5 minutes. Add pepper to taste and a few strips of red sweet pepper for colour, if desired. Serve immediately.

Potato Maroc

More than just a potato salad; the Moroccans perform miracles with the humble spud. **Heart Foundation approved**

Serves 4-6

INGREDIENTS
1 kg potatoes
A little grapeseed oil

DRESSING
4 Tbsp virgin olive oil
1½ Tbsp vinegar
2 Tbsp finely grated onion
2 Tbsp finely chopped flat-leafed parsley
¼ tspn paprika
¼ tspn chilli powder
Freshly ground black pepper

METHOD

Cook the potatoes in their skins in boiling water until just tender. Drain and peel while still hot. Brush with grapeseed oil and allow to cool. When cold, dice. Mix all the dressing ingredients in a small bowl. Toss with potatoes and chill.

Potato Salad with Cumin

This potato salad probably originated in North Africa where cumin and potatoes grow plentifully. We tend to think of potato salads as heavy fillers, however this one is light. **Heart Foundation Approved.**

Serves 4

INGREDIENTS
700g baby potatoes
$^1/_8$ to ¼ tspn cayenne pepper to taste
1 tspn ground cumin
1 tspn olive oil
Juice of 1 large lemon
3 Tbsp plain low-fat yoghurt
2 Tbsp fresh, chopped coriander, or fresh, chopped parsley

METHOD
Steam or boil the potatoes until tender (15 to 20 minutes). Wash in chilled water and drain. Combine the cayenne pepper, cumin, olive oil, lemon juice, and yoghurt in a bowl and mix well. Toss with potatoes. Serve warm or chilled, sprinkled with the fresh coriander. This potato salad will keep for 2 to 3 days in the fridge as long as you haven't topped with the coriander.

Courgette Salad

The squash family includes pumpkins, cucumbers, marrows, courgette, and, of course, squash. This recipe uses courgette to make a stunningly simple salad. In traditional Mediterranean recipes for this kind of salad, pine nuts would be used, but I find a few chopped pecan nuts are even better.
Heart Foundation approved.

Serves 4

INGREDIENTS
50g pecan or pine nuts
3 Tbsp extra virgin olive oil
500g small courgettes, sliced
50g currants
½ salad onion, finely chopped
1 clove garlic, peeled
2 Tbsp lemon juice
2 tsp balsamic or other wine vinegar
1 Tbsp chopped parsley leaves, preferably Italian parsley
1 Tbsp chopped mint leaves
Pepper to taste

METHOD
In a frying pan, dry toast the nuts by tossing for 1-2 minutes over medium heat. Remove from pan and set aside. Add 1 Tbsp olive oil to the pan. Add courgettes and cook, tossing, until just brown. A few seconds before they're done, toss in the currants — these add a delightful sweetness to the salad. Then add the chopped onion. Remove from pan and cool. Prepare a salad bowl by rubbing it with the clove of peeled garlic. For the dressing, vigorously whisk together the lemon juice, vinegar, remaining olive oil, parsley and mint and season to taste with pepper. (If more liquid is needed, add

more lemon juice). Put half the dressing mixture in the salad bowl and reserve the rest. Swirl salad bowl to coat with dressing. Add the nuts and the courgette mixture to the bowl. Pour remaining dressing over salad and toss well.

Leftover potential: Keeps for 24 hours in the refrigerator.

Hint: When buying courgette, check that they are firm and not soft, bandy or shrivelled. To prepare, cut them into rings about 1cm thick.

Thai'd Up Prawn Salad

A light, but nourishing salad with a hint of chilli. A little sweet and sour miracle, that's made in no time and is wonderful served warm or cold. **Heart Foundation approved.**

Serves 4

INGREDIENTS
425g Australian canned peach slices, well drained
½ red sweet pepper
1 tsp sesame oil
1 Tbsp chopped coriander leaves
Small piece lemon grass stem, crushed and chopped (optional)
1 tsp finely chopped or minced ginger
2 tsp sweet chilli sauce
1 Tbsp fish sauce (or reduced salt soya sauce)
1 Tbsp lime or lemon juice
1 Tbsp unsalted peanuts
750g large prawns, cooked and shelled
2 Tbsp chopped spring onions
Lettuce leaves (preferably a soft-leafed variety but not iceberg!)
Extra coriander leaves for garnish

METHOD

Dice one third of peaches. Chop sweet pepper into a small dice. Heat sesame oil in a frying pan over medium heat, add lemon grass (if using) and ginger, and stir-fry for 1 minute. Mix in chilli sauce, fish sauce and lime or lemon juice. Mix sweet pepper and diced peaches with coriander leaves and ginger mixture. In a frying pan over medium heat, lightly toast the peanuts. Add the prawns and cook, tossing, for a few seconds to warm. The prawns should not overcook. Put lettuce leaves in a salad bowl, then add prawn and vegetable mixtures, toss and garnish with spring onions, remaining peach slices and extra coriander. Serve slightly warm.

Leftover potential: Keeps for a couple of hours.

Pat Cash Pasta Salad

Pat Cash is a sportsman who takes his eating very seriously. He eats little red meat, fats, oils or sugar, which probably accounts for the reason his body fat is less than 7%. (We should all be so fortunate). I created this recipe based on what he told me were his favourite foods. I used pumpkin pasta in the prototype, but any pasta would do.

Heart Foundation approved

Serves 4

INGREDIENTS
1 Tbsp olive oil
1 small aubergine, diced and pre-salted (see hint below)
1 small courgette, diced
1 young leek, finely sliced

Juice of 1 orange
3 or 4 asparagus spears, cut in half
½ cup sugar snap peas or mange tout, trimmed
2 large ripe salad tomatoes
250g cooked pasta (preferably fetuccine/tagliatelle)
2 Tbsp roasted hazelnuts
1 Tbsp finely chopped basil leaves
1 Tbsp finely chopped coriander leaves
1 tsp ground coriander

Dressing
2 Tbsp lime or lemon juice
2 tsp sweet chilli sauce
½ tsp sesame oil

METHOD

Heat olive oil in a non-stick frying pan and stir-fry aubergine for about 5 minutes, or until softened. Gently poach courgette and leek slices in orange juice for 5 minutes. Drain. Blanch asparagus and peas in boiling water for 30 seconds, then immediately transfer to cold water to set the colour. Peel tomato, remove seeds and dice flesh finely. Place all salad ingredients in a salad bowl. *To make dressing*: Whisk together lime or lemon juice, chilli sauce and sesame oil. Pour over salad and toss.

Leftover potential: Keeps a day in the refrigerator.

Hint: To prepare aubergine, sprinkle with salt and stand in a colander for at least 30 minutes. Rinse under cold water drain, and dry on paper towels.

Lemony Mixed Vegetables

The perfect accompaniment to many meat dishes, the traditional *mirepoix* mixture of carrots, onions, leek and celery is cooked in wine and stock and served in a subtle lemon-flavoured sauce. **Heart Foundation approved.**

Serves 6

INGREDIENTS
2 leeks, finely sliced
4 Tbsp good olive oil
2 medium onions, finely chopped
2 medium carrots, finely diced
2 sticks celery, finely diced
500ml dry white wine
500ml chicken, veal or vegetable stock
6 tsp lemon juice
4 egg yolks
2 tsp cornflour
½ tsp white pepper

METHOD
Into a heavy-based, deep saucepan, gently cook the leeks n the olive oil for 5 minutes, stirring frequently. Stir in onions, carrots and celery and cook for about 2 minutes longer. Add wine and stock, reduce heat and cook for a further 15 minutes. Just before serving, whisk lemon juice with egg yolks, then stir in cornflour and white pepper. Slowly stir 2 Tbsp vegetable liquid into the egg yolk mixture. When well mixed, stir egg mixture into the vegetables to make a light lemon sauce.

❦

Serving suggestion: Especially recommended as a partner for Herbed Lamb Balls

Leftover potential: Keeps up to two days in the refrigerator.

Roasted Toms

Now that sun dried tomatoes have become passé, here's a great alternative — tomatoes slow-roasted in the oven with herbs. I like to use the hardy herbs such as thyme, rosemary and oregano. They are rich in oils and are usually in plentiful supply. They are discarded after use. **Heart Foundation approved.**

INGREDIENTS
1 kg ripe tomatoes
2 Tbsp extra virgin olive oil
1 Tbsp raw sugar
1 tsp black pepper
Bunches of thyme, rosemary and oregano

METHOD
Lightly oil a baking tray. Cut tomatoes in half and place cut side up on the prepared tray. Drizzle tomatoes with olive oil and sprinkle with sugar and pepper. Top tomatoes with generous amounts of herbs it's really hard to overdo it. Roast at 150°C for at least 1½ hours. Serve hot from the oven, or cold in salads.

Leftover potential: Roasted tomatoes keep for two or three days in the refrigerator.

Stuffed Artichokes

This old Sicilian recipe turns four artichokes into a decent self-contained meal. **Heart Foundation approved.**
Serves 4

INGREDIENTS
4 large, fresh artichokes
1 Tbsp olive oil
1 medium onion, finely chopped
2 cloves garlic, finely chopped
1 litre tomato pulp or crushed canned tomatoes
2 cups fresh breadcrumbs
1 cup parsley, finely chopped
50g parmesan cheese
2 large eggs
Pepper to taste
2 Tbsp stock
1 Tbsp tomato concentrate (paste)
Lemon juice

METHOD
Trim top and bottom of artichokes and remove bottom, outer leaves. Set aside. Heat oil in a large saucepan and cook half the onion and half the garlic for 2 minutes, making sure the garlic does not burn. Add the tomato pulp and cook for 10 minutes. Meanwhile, make a stuffing by mixing together the bread-crumbs, parsley, parmesan cheese, eggs, pepper to taste and the remaining onion and garlic. Mix in stock to make a thick paste. If it's too sloppy, add more breadcrumbs. To prepare artichokes: Open up

centre and scrape out the choke (the fibrous flower in the middle of the artichoke), taking care not to scrape away too much of the heart. Squeeze a little lemon juice into the centre to prevent discoloration. Now starting from the outer leaves, pull each leaf away from centre, far enough to insert a little of the stuffing mixture. Work your way around and up the artichoke, finishing off by packing stuffing into the centre. Arrange artichokes snugly in a saucepan. Spoon over the freshly made tomato sauce. Put the lid on the pan and simmer for 1 hour for medium artichokes or 1½ hours for large ones. Serve topped with a little of the tomato sauce.

Leftover potential: Poor. Eat as soon as they're cooked.
Hint: Any remaining sauce is delicious served over pasta to create an artichoke flavoured delight.

Leek and Ham Gratin

A dish I learnt to prepare in Belgium. Pieces of cooked leek are wrapped in ham, then covered with a spicy cheese sauce. In Belgium, it is usually made with *witloof* or Belgian endive. I find the leek is a subtler alternative, without the bitterness which comes with the endive. The bed of mashed potato is optional but makes for a more substantial dish.

Serves 4

INGREDIENTS
4 leeks
3 tsp lemon juice
50g butter or margarine

50g plain flour
500ml milk
125g grated Swiss cheese (or other)
½ tsp grated nutmeg
¼ tsp paprika
2 Tbsp chopped parsley (optional)
1 egg yolk
Mashed potato (optional)
200g lean ham slices
1 egg white
Parmesan cheese
Breadcrumbs

METHOD

Trim the leeks, removing the leafy top and the bottom. Cut a cross in the tops, plunge into cold water and soak to remove any soil. Put leeks in a saucepan, cover with water, add 2 tsp lemon juice and simmer for about 30 minutes, or until cooked. Do not boil too rapidly or the leeks will break up. Meanwhile, make a cheese sauce by melting the butter or margarine in a medium saucepan, then stir in the flour and cook gently for 3 minutes. Add the milk, a little at a time, stirring frequently, until sauce thickens. Stir in the cheese, nutmeg, paprika and parsley (if using). When the cheese has melted and the sauce is smooth, remove from heat and whisk in the egg yolk. Drain the leeks well and cool a little before assembling the dish. Spread a layer of mashed potato, if using, over the base of an ovenproof dish. Roll leeks in ham slices, cutting the leeks into shorter lengths if they are too long. Place ham wrapped leeks in the ovenproof dish and top with half the sauce. Beat egg white with the remaining lemon juice until stiff peaks form. Fold egg white into the remaining sauce. Spoon over leeks, then sprinkle with a little Parmesan cheese and a few breadcrumbs. Bake at 190°C for 25-30 minutes or until top is beautifully browned.
Leftover potential: Keeps for two or three days in the refrigerator.

Fish and Seafood

Fish continue to frighten people. I don't mean sharks and piranhas, but the every day fish that stares up at you from the fishmonger's slab. I am sure that part of the fear comes from the challenge presented in preparing fish for cooking, yet it is as easy to deal with as meat. And it is in plentiful supply in Ireland and Britain. Although it is rarely as cheap as meat, it may be enjoyed in smaller quantities and it is certainly more economical to buy whole fish than fillets.

Nutritionists recommend we eat fish at least three times a week because it is a good balance of protein and fat. A few fishy tips:

Buying. Look the fish in the eye. It should be bright and bulging out, not sunken. The flesh should be firm and smell fresh and saline (if it is a sea fish). There should be no smell of ammonia. The scales should be firmly attached and the gills should be red.

Frozen fish. Today it is possible to buy fish caught yesterday several thousand kilometres away. It is snap frozen on the boat as soon as it is caught. However, it is unwise to freeze fish in a conventional domestic freezer since it freezes slowly causing ice crystals to form in the flesh. This damages its texture. Always allow fish to thaw slowly. Dry thoroughly before cooking.

To scale a fish. Remove the fins with a small sharp knife. Holding the tail, scrape the scales away from you down towards the head. Make sure all scales are removed then wash and dry the fish. If the fish is slimy pour boiling water over it, drain and then it will be easier to scale.

Cleaning. You will normally buy the fish without entrails. Nevertheless it is a good idea to wash the interior of the fish with salted water and dry with kitchen towel.

Moroccan Fish

One of the principal mixtures which gives a distinctive flavour to Moroccan savoury cooking is chermoula, a blend of spices, herbs, onion, lemon juice and oil. It works well for both fish and meats. The quantities of spices given are suitable for most purposes, but can be adjusted to suit your taste after you've tried it. **Heart Foundation approved.**

Serves 4

INGREDIENTS
1 tsp ground coriander
½ tsp ground cinnamon
1 tsp ground cumin
1 tsp ground paprika
1 tsp ground ginger
1 small onion, finely chopped
4 cloves garlic, finely chopped
1 Tbsp parsley (preferably Italian), finely chopped
1 Tbsp fresh coriander, finely chopped
1 small chilli, seeds removed, finely chopped (or you could use chilli sauce)
A few strands of saffron (optional)
2 Tbsp lemon juice
3 Tbsp nut oil, such as macadamia oil (or other oil of your choice can be used)
4 fish fillets or cutlets

METHOD
Make a chermoula by mixing together the spices in bowl grinding them if they are not powdery. Add all remaining ingredients except fish and oil. Slowly dribble in oil, a little at a time, stirring constantly (as if making mayonnaise). Continue adding oil until

all has been incorporated. Rub fish with the chermoula and marinate for at least 1 hour. Pan fry fish, preferably in a non-stick pan. Even in other frying pans the oil in the chermoula should be enough to prevent the fish from sticking.

Serving suggestion: I like to serve this dish with couscous made up according to instructions on the packet.

Leftover potential: Chermoula keeps for several days in the refrigerator.

Pickled Sardines with Aioli

Fresh sardines are lightly pickled and served with the French provincial mayonnaise, Aioli. The recipe could also be made with other small fish fillets, such as herring or whiting. **Heart Foundation approved**.

Serves 4

INGREDIENTS
500g fresh sardine fillets
Pickling mixture
4 Tbsp lemon juice
2 Tbsp mild vinegar
1 tsp sugar
1 Tbsp chopped oregano leaves (or 1 tsp dried oregano)
Aioli
2 cloves garlic
2 Tbsp basil leaves (optional)
1 large egg yolk
1 tsp Dijon style mustard
2 tsp lemon juice
250ml oil (walnut, macadamia or olive)

METHOD
For picking mixture: Whisk together pickling ingredients. Put a layer of fillets in a non-reactive dish and cover with pickling mixture. Repeat process finishing with generous amount of mixture. Refrigerate for at least 30 minutes (more if you are using bigger fish).

For aioli: In a mortar (or food processor) crush garlic. Add basil (if using), egg yolk, mustard and lemon juice. Blend well. Slowly add oil, a drop at a time, stirring constantly. Continue adding oil and stirring until a thick cream is formed.

Drain sardines and serve with a little of the aioli.

Serving suggestion: Serve sardines with a salad of mixed lettuces and good bread.

Leftover potential: Keeps well for two or three days in refrigerator.

Hint: If the aioli mixture curdles, start with another egg and add the curdled mixture, a little at a time, stirring in constantly until blended.

Ginger Fish Sauna

One of my favourite ways of dealing with a whole fish. It is steamed over a spicy ginger liquor, which then becomes a tasty sauce. **Heart Foundation approved.**

Serves 4

INGREDIENTS
1 whole fish about 1.5kg, cleaned and scaled
1 Tbsp turmeric
1 x 5cm piece of ginger, crushed
Juice and pared rind of 1 orange

750ml fish or chicken stock
1 Tbsp reduced salt soya sauce
3 cardamom pods, crushed
1 tsp chopped or minced ginger
1 tsp minced chilli
2 tsp peanut butter
2 Tbsp coconut milk (optional)
1 Tbsp chopped spring onions, white part only
¼ sweet pepper, cut into thin strips
1 Tbsp peanuts
1 tsp sesame oil
1 Tbsp chopped spring onions, green part only

METHOD

Pat fish dry with paper towels. Cut a few slashes in the fish on each side. Place turmeric in a plastic bag and shake to distribute evenly. Put fish in the bag and shake to cover with turmeric. Remove fish from the bag. Place the crushed ginger and orange rind in the body cavity. In a wok large enough to hold the fish, put the orange juice, stock, soya sauce, cardamom pods, chopped or minced ginger and chilli. Put chopsticks across the wok to hold the fish or you could use a wire rack. Place the fish on the chopsticks or rack. Cover with lid or aluminium foil and steam for 30-40 minutes. Remember to allow longer if the fish has come directly out of the refrigerator. To check if fish is cooked, insert a knife into the flesh. When it flakes and comes away from the bone, it is cooked. When cooked, remove fish from the wok and put in a warm place.

Remove rack from wok and cook steaming liquor to reduce to one third of its volume. Remove cardamom pods. Stir in the peanut butter and coconut milk (if using) and heat. Do not allow the mixture to boil once the coconut milk is added. Briefly fry white parts of spring onions, sweet pepper and peanuts in the sesame oil. Serve fish topped with the sauce, sweet pepper mixture and green parts of spring onions.

Serving suggestion: Delicious served with boiled brown rice and stir-fried vegetables.

Leftover potential: Best eaten immediately, or cold on the same day.

Fish Cakes with Cucumber Relish

Thai-style fish cakes that don't have the texture of squash balls, as they so often do in restaurants. These light delights are served with a sweet and sour cucumber relish. **Heart Foundation approved**.

INGREDIENTS
1 chilli, seeded (or 1 tsp minced chilli)
2 Tbsp red sweet pepper flesh, chopped
2 cloves garlic, minced or finely chopped
1 tsp chopped lemon grass stem (optional)
1 Kaffir lime leaf, finely chopped
2 tsp fish sauce
1 large egg
300g white fish fillets
6 stringless beans, finely chopped
1 Tbsp cornflour
Peanut oil for cooking

For the cucumber relish
4 Tbsp rice vinegar (or good white wine vinegar)
1 Tbsp water
1 heaped Tbsp caster sugar
1 Lebanese cucumber, peeled, seeds removed and finely chopped
1 chilli, seeded (or 1 tsp minced chilli)

2 Tbsp roasted peanuts, chopped
1 Tbsp chopped coriander leaves

METHOD
To make the fish cakes: Process chilli, sweet pepper, garlic, lemon grass (if using), lime leaf and fish sauce either in a food processor or by grinding in a mortar. Mix in the egg. Pat fish dry and check for bones, removing if necessary. Finely chop fish and add to egg mixture. Stir in beans and cornflour. Set aside for about 1 hour. Shape fish mixture into patties. Brush fryingpan with a little oil and cook patties for 4-5 minutes each side.To make the relish: In a non-reactive saucepan put vinegar, water and sugar, and heat to dissolve sugar. Taste for sweetness. If relish is too acidic, add more sugar. Cool. Add remaining ingredients. Serve with fish cakes. Leftover potential: Does not keep well.

Fish and Vegetable Stir-fry

A recipe provided by Bettina Jenkins of the Sydney Fish Market's Seafood School. It is a high protein dish which is low in fat and salt. Bettina uses Trevally fillets, but any firm white fish fillets will work well in this simple dish. The vegetables are suggestions only. Feel free to experiment with your favourite vegetables. Heart Foundation approved.

Serves 4

INGREDIENTS
500g fish fillets
2 tsp oil such as peanut, canola or olive
¼ tsp sesame oil

1 clove garlic, crushed
1 tsp curry powder (optional)
½ cup broccoli florets
50g snow peas
¼ cup sliced red sweet pepper
1 medium carrot, cut into julienne strips
1 tsp cornflour
½ cup chicken stock
2 tsp reduced salt soya sauce
2 spring onions, chopped

METHOD

Cut fish into cubes or thickish strips. Heat oils together in wok or large frying pan. Add garlic and curry powder (if using), and stir-fry for 30 seconds over high heat. Add fish and cook for about 1 minute or until fish is half cooked. Add all the vegetables, except the spring onions, and stir-fry for 1 minute. Blend cornflour with the stock and soya sauce. Add to the fish and vegetables and cook, stirring constantly, until sauce thickens. Add spring onions and serve.

Serving suggestion: For a complete meal, serve with boiled white or brown rice or Chinese noodles.
Leftover potential: May be eaten cold.

Orange Prawns with Noodles

Due to the acidity of the sauce, make it in a non-reactive pan. **Heart Foundation approved.**

Serves 4

INGREDIENTS
750ml orange juice
750ml low salt fish or chicken stock
2 tsp wine vinegar
2 Tbsp finely chopped carrot
2 Tbsp finely chopped celery
2 Tbsp finely sliced leek
2 Tbsp finely chopped onion
500g large prawns in their shells
1 Tbsp olive oil
1 x 375g packet egg noodles, boiled but still *al dente*
Pepper to taste

METHOD

In a large, non-reactive saucepan, put orange juice, stock, wine vinegar and 1 Tbsp of each of the carrot, celery, leek and onion. Reserve the rest for later use. Cook the vegetables over medium heat for 25 minutes.

Meanwhile, peel the prawns and put the shells and heads in the pan with the vegetables so that they contribute their flavour. Once all have been peeled, cut along the back of each prawn and remove the dark intestinal tract, rinse and dry on paper towels. Cook prawns lightly in olive oil for about 1 minute. They don't need to cook right through at this stage and it is important the prawns aren't overcooked. Transfer to a warm place. Strain stock mixture, discarding the prawn shells, heads and vegetables. Return strained stock to the pan, add remaining vegetables and cook until the stock mixture reduces and is of a syrupy consistency, and the vegetables are softened. Remove pan from the heat. Stir in the prawns and the freshly cooked, but still warm, noodles. Season to taste.

Leftover potential: May be reheated the same day, but I wouldn't recommend keeping it beyond that.

Ravioli of Lobster with Tomato and Basil sauce

One of my favourite recipes from Tetsuya Wakuda's award-winning Sydney restaurant uses fresh seafood in an innovative Japanese/Australian way. Quite involved but worth the effort.

Serves 6

INGREDIENTS
For the ravioli
200g scallop meat, chilled
½ tsp tarragon, finely chopped
1 Tbsp chopped chives
1 egg white
300ml cream, chilled
200g chilled green lobster meat, finely chopped
Salt and pepper to taste
24 Gow Gee skins (available from Oriental food shops)
24 squares of Nori cut into 2cm squares (available from Oriental food shops)
Wakame and Ogo seaweeds and flying fish roe (available from Japanese food shops), for garnish

For the sauce
100ml extra virgin olive oil
8 Tbsp peeled and diced tomato
1½ Tbsp rice vinegar
1 tsp ground coriander
½ tsp finely chopped basil leaves
½ tsp finely chopped garlic
Salt and pepper
Pinch of sugar

METHOD

To make ravioli filling: Place scallops, tarragon, chives and egg white in food processor and blend to make a smooth paste. With the processor still running, gradually add the chilled cream in a steady stream. When the cream has been assimilated, mix the paste with the lobster and salt and pepper. Cover and chill until needed. To assemble ravioli: Lay out 12 Gow Gee skins and lay a Nori sheet on each. Place a spoonful of the seafood filling on top, cover with another Nori square and then another Gow Gee skin. Gently wet the edges and press together to seal. Poach ravioli for about 5 minutes in a large saucepan of simmering salted water to which a dash of vegetable oil has been added.

To make sauce: Mix sauce ingredients together.

To serve: On a warm plate spread some Wakame, then top with ravioli and sauce and garnish with Ogo and flying fish roe.

Leftover potential: There will be no leftovers!

Hint: To keep seafood and cream icy-cold while preparing other ingredients, place over a bowl of ice.

Poultry

These days when we talk of poultry we usually mean chicken unless we are talking turkey, which is still a once-a-year treat for most of us. The chicken was first domesticated in India, where its ancestor was the wild red jungle fowl, *Gallus gallus* . Apparently, these birds were shy and easily angered and were regarded as sacred. They appeared in religious ceremonies at which their entrails were examined in search of the meaning of life. It's no wonder they were easily angered.

Recipes using chicken were first published as far back as Roman times in the writings of Apicius, one of the earliest foodies. Since then chicken has become the world's most popular source of meat. The reasons for its popularity are price and versatility. Chicken is inexpensive and there are very few meat dishes that cannot be made with its meat. It is also a great source of protein, iron, zinc and riboflavin. Most of the fat is in the skin so it's a good idea to remove it before cooking. I prefer fresh birds to the frozen variety. When selecting a chicken, the meat should be firm and the point of the breastbone should be soft and flexible. Remove plastic wrapping as soon as you get the bird home. Wipe dry with paper towel and store loosely covered in the refrigerator. Since poultry is susceptible to bacteria, make sure it is handled with washed hands, use clean equipment and wash it and your hands after handling. You should make it a rule never to handle raw and cooked chicken at the same time. Before cooking the chicken should be allowed to warm to room temperature that includes frozen birds, which should be thoroughly thawed. If stuffing the chicken, it is a good idea always to do it just before cooking, especially if the stuffing is warm when placed inside the bird. Allow extra cooking time for a stuffed chicken.

Chicken Pecan Terrine

The terrine is named after the French earthenware dish that is used for both cooking and serving. A terrine may be made with either meat, fish, vegetables or even fruits This terrine is made with chicken, pecan nuts and grille sweet peppers and seasoned with spices. **Heart Foundation approved.**

Serves 8

INGREDIENTS

3 or 4 red or yellow sweet peppers
250g skinless chicken breast or thigh meat minced or finely chopped
50g pecan nuts, finely chopped
1 large egg, lightly beaten
1 medium onion, finely chopped
1 small carrot, grated
1 tsp mixed spice
½ tsp black pepper
2 Tbsp strong chicken stock
5 or 6 juniper berries, finely chopped (optional)
1 Tbsp brandy (optional)
Breadcrumbs (preferably freshly made)
3 or 4 bacon rashers, rind and fat removed
50g whole pecan nuts
250g skinless chicken breast cut into strips

METHOD

First prepare the sweet peppers by cutting slices of flesh away from the seeds and discarding the stalk. Place skin side up on an oiled baking tray. Grill until skin blackens. Remove sweet pepper pieces from baking tray and place in a plastic bag. Tie top of bag and leave to cool. Once they are cool the skins are easily removed. In a large bowl mix minced chicken, chopped pecan nuts, egg, onion, carrot, mixed spice, pepper, stock and juniper berries and brandy (if using). Mix well, then slowly add breadcrumbs to make a reasonably firm mixture. Oil a 10 x 15cm terrine or other ovenproof dish and put down a layer of bacon rashers. Add one third of the chicken mixture, packing down well on top of the bacon. Add a layer of whole pecans, followed by a layer of chicken strips. Add a layer of sweet pepper and repeat the whole process, finishing with a layer of the chicken mixture. Cover dish with aluminium foil and stand in a roasting pan with enough water in it to come halfway up sides of the dish. Cook at 190°C for 2 hours. Cool terrine completely then refrigerate before serving.

Serving suggestion: I serve this terrine with citrus and onion chutney (see recipe below).

Leftover potential: Keeps for a week in the refrigerator.

Onion and Citrus Chutney

This tangy concoction is best made with kumquats, but since they're rarely available, you could use either orange or mandarin segments. It's best made in a pan which won't react with the acid in the orange and vinegar (stainless steel or enamel). Serve with patés, terrines, etc. Try it with Chicken and Pecan Terrine **Heart Foundation approved**.

INGREDIENTS
2 medium onions, finely chopped
1 Tbsp oil
¼ cup sugar
1 cup orange segments, kumquat slices or canned mandarin pieces
Juice of 1 orange

2 Tbsp good wine vinegar
½ tsp ground coriander
½ tsp ground ginger
Pinch of pepper

METHOD
Cook onions in oil over medium heat for about 5 minutes or until onions soften. Stir in sugar and keep cooking for about 10 minutes longer or until mixture starts to brown. Add citrus fruit, orange juice, wine vinegar, coriander, ginger and pepper. Continue cooking, uncovered, until mixture reaches a jam-like consistency. Check that the chutney is not too sharp and, if it is, add more sugar. Allow to cool.

Hint: Keeps for several days in an airtight container in the refrigerator.

Chicken Waterzooi

Based on the national dish of Belgium, this chicken casserole benefits from the addition of one of the world's most useful fruits, the lemon. **Heart Foundation approved**.
Serves 4

INGREDIENTS
4 chicken pieces, skinned
750ml low-salt chicken stock
1 medium onion, chopped finely
Small sprig parsley
Small sprig thyme
2 bay leaves

3 juniper berries, crushed
½ tsp grated nutmeg
2 sticks celery, sliced
2 young leeks, sliced
2 medium carrots, grated
2 cloves garlic, finely chopped
2 egg yolks, lightly beaten
1 Tbsp cornflour
1 tsp Dijon mustard
Juice and grated rind of 1 large lemon

METHOD

In a large saucepan, put chicken pieces, stock, onion, herbs, juniper berries, nutmeg and half the celery, leeks and carrots. If the stock does not cover ingredients, add water until all ingredients are covered and simmer for about 1 hour or until chicken falls off the bone. Drain chicken and keep warm. Strain cooking liquid back into the saucepan. Add remaining celery, leeks, carrots, and garlic and cook, uncovered, for 30 minutes or until reduced to half the volume of strained liquid. Just before serving, remove chicken meat from bone.

Mix together egg yolks, cornflour and mustard. Slowly mix in lemon juice and rind. Stir in reduced stock, a spoonful at a time, until about 500ml is added, then pour this mixture back into the reduced stock. Cook, stirring constantly, for about 1 minute, or until sauce thickens. Arrange chicken on warm serving plates and pour over the thick sauce with its vegetables.

Serving suggestion: For a complete meal accompany with wholemeal rolls, or boiled rice or pasta.

Leftover potential: Keeps for two or three days in the refrigerator.

Chicken with Tangy Plum Sauce

A hint of the Orient with this simple main course recipe. **Heart Foundation approved.**

Serves 4

INGREDIENTS

2-3 rashers bacon, rind and fat removed, cut into strips
2 Tbsp olive oil
750g chicken leg pieces or thigh fillets, skinned
1 medium onion, finely sliced
1 tsp minced or finely chopped garlic
1 tsp minced or finely chopped ginger
500ml low, salt chicken stock or consommé
825g can Australian plums, drained, halved and stoned
1 Tbsp chopped fresh parsley
2 tsp Dijon-style mustard
Pepper to taste

METHOD

In a large frying pan, cook bacon in half the olive oil over medium heat for 1 minute. Add chicken and brown all over. Remove bacon and chicken from pan. Put remaining olive oil in pan, add onion, garlic and ginger and cook for 1-2 minutes. Add chicken stock, plums, parsley, mustard and pepper and cook vigorously, stirring frequently, for 15 minutes to reduce mixture. The mixture should reduce to about one-third of its original volume to make a thickish sauce. Reduce heat, return chicken and bacon to pan. Turn chicken to coat with the sauce and simmer gently for 40 minutes, turning chicken occasionally.

Serving suggestion: Serve with pasta or rice.

Leftover potential: May be reheated.

Note: If a thicker sauce is required, remove chicken pieces and cook the sauce for 5-6 minutes longer or until reduced to the desired consistency.

Hunter Chicken

Mushrooms, onions and wine form the basis of the classic French sauce, Chasseur or hunter sauce, so-called because this sauce works extremely well with any game meat. It also goes beautifully with chicken, as in the *Consuming Passions* Hunter Chicken recipe. I allow a Maryland cut of chicken per person that's the thigh and drumstick. **Heart Foundation approved.**

Serves 4

INGREDIENTS
4 chicken Maryland pieces, skinned
2 Tbsp olive oil
2 Tbsp brandy
4 Tbsp chopped onions (preferably shallots)
150g chopped mushrooms (preferably wild)
500ml veal or chicken stock
300ml white wine (preferably Chardonnay)
2 bay leaves
1-2 sprigs thyme
1-2 sprigs parsley
2 tsp tomato paste

METHOD

Brown chicken pieces in 1 Tbsp oil in a large saucepan over high heat. Warm the brandy and flame the chicken. Once the flames have died down, remove chicken pieces, add onion and cook for 5 minutes. Remove onion and set aside. Put remaining oil in pan, add mushrooms and cook for 2 minutes. Toss them around, and if they get too dry don't add any more oil. Instead, just add a little stock, making sure the mushrooms don't start stewing.

Remove mushrooms. Into the pan put the stock, wine and herbs (tied together with butcher's string). Add the tomato paste and reduce liquid until syrupy and about half its original volume. Return chicken, onions and mushrooms to pan. Cover, reduce the heat and cook very, very, very slowly for about 1 hour.

Serving suggestion: Serve Hunter Chicken with plain noodles and a dark green vegetable.

Leftover potential: Keeps well in the refrigerator for two or three days.

Grape Chicken Idea

Based on a Lebanese recipe, this dish combines the fruitiness of grapes, with the sourness of wine vinegar and a bold blend of herbs and spices. **Heart Foundation approved.**

Serves 4

INGREDIENTS
1 Tbsp macadamia, walnut or almond oil
½ tsp ground cinnamon
½ tsp ground nutmeg
2 or 3 cloves
150g seedless grapes, washed

250ml fruity white wine
1 Tbsp good white wine vinegar (or red wine vinegar for a darker
sauce)
2 Tbsp chicken stock
500g skinned and boned chicken thigh meat
1 Tbsp finely chopped onion
2 Tbsp almond meal
Pepper to taste
2 tsp chopped fresh marjoram or thyme (or ½ tsp dried thyme)
¼ tsp chilli powder (optional)
1 or 2 Tbsp blanched almonds to serve

METHOD

Heat oil in a frying pan over medium heat. Add cinnamon, nutmeg and cloves and sizzle for few seconds. Remove cloves. Add whole grapes and cook for 2 minutes. Add wine, vinegar and stock and cook for about 10 minutes, or until reduced by half. Meanwhile, open out the chicken pieces and lay each on a length of butcher's (or other cotton) string. Top with a little onion, almond meal, pepper, marjoram or thyme and chilli powder, if using. Pat down. Roll up and tie each into a parcel, then nestle in the reduced sauce. Sprinkle remaining almond meal and onion into the sauce. Cover pan and simmer very slowly for about 30 minutes, turning the parcels after 15 minutes. Dry toast the blanched almonds for about 1 minute over medium heat, or until just browned. Once cooked, remove chicken and keep warm. Reduce sauce to a syrupy consistency over medium heat. Serve parcels with sauce and topped with blanched almonds.

Leftover potential Keeps two or three days in the refrigerator.

Olive Focaccia.

Twice-cooked Kervella Goats Cheese Souffle and Fondues Bruxelloises.

Courgette Salad, Pat Cash Pasta Salad and Roasted Toms.

Ricotta and Spinach Cannelloni, Broccoli Pasta and Mushroom Magic.

Stuffed Artichokes and Leek and Ham Gratin.

Ginger Fish Sauna and Moroccan Fish.

Chicken Prawn Fandango and Chicken Chardonnay.

Chicken Waterzooi and Hunter Chicke

Chicken Pecan Terrine, Onion and Citrus Chutney, Chicken with Tangy Plum Sauce.

erbed Lamb Balls, Lambshank and Tomato Ragu.

Pork and Apple Pie, Apple and Orange Sauce and Apricot Herb Stuffed Pork Loin.

Sweet Pepper Pork and Spicy Spare Ribs.

Peach and Pecan Pizza, Pears in Dessert Wine Sauce and Fruit Flamri.

Nightingales Nest and Ginger Delight.

Fruit Compote, Almond Pudding and Nut Crunchie.

Chicken and Leek Pancakes

A terrific dish which may be made in advance. Pancakes are stuffed with a chicken and leek mixture, topped with a light sauce and parmesan cheese and baked to perfection. **Heart Foundation approved.**

Serves 4

INGREDIENTS
Light flavoured oil such as canola, peanut or extra light olive oil

For the pancake batter
75g plain flour
75g self-raising flour
2 large eggs
125ml reduced fat milk
125ml water

For the filling and topping
300g skinless chicken breast
600ml plus 2 Tbsp low-salt chicken stock
1 tender leek, cleaned and finely sliced
1 Tbsp cornflour
Pepper to taste
1 Tbsp grated parmesan cheese
1 Tbsp fresh breadcrumbs

METHOD
Make the pancake batter by mixing the two flours with the eggs, then adding the milk and water. Stir well, but don't overwork or the pancakes will be tough. Stand for 30 minutes to allow the starch grains to swell. Gently poach the chicken breasts in the 600ml of

stock for 10 minutes, or until cooked. In a separate saucepan, poach leek slices for 10-15 minutes in remaining 2 Tbsp of stock to soften. If the leek starts to stick, add more stock. Cook pancakes, preferably in non-stick pan with a little oil (which provides texture and allows the pancakes to brown well). Don't be alarmed if the first couple stick. They usually do for me! As the pancakes are cooked, stack on top of each other.

Remove chicken from stock. Keep stock and simmer until reduced to $^3/_4$ cup. Cut chicken into small pieces. Make a sauce by mixing the cornflour with 1 Tbsp of cold water, then slowly stir in reduced stock, a spoonful at a time. You should have a sauce the consistency of smooth custard. If it's too thick add a little milk. If it's too thin reduce it over medium heat. Divide sauce into two lots. Mix the chicken and the leek into one lot of sauce and season to taste. Put a spoonful of chicken mixture on each pancake and roll up. Place pancakes side by side in a greased baking dish. Pour over remaining sauce. Sprinkle with parmesan cheese and breadcrumbs and bake at 200°C for 10 minutes, or until top is brown.

Serving suggestion: For a complete meal, accompany with a salad of mixed lettuces and herbs.
Leftover potential: Poor.
Hint: If making the dish in advance and refrigerating, cook in oven at 180°C for 30 minutes before increasing temperature and browning.

Chicken Prawn Fandango

The Spanish acknowledge it with their Paella, as do the Chinese with a variety of dishes that chicken combines well with seafood, as it does in this colourful concoction. Though the fandango is a Spanish dance, this dish owes more to Oriental cuisine. **Heart Foundation approved.**

Serves 4

INGREDIENTS
300g skinless, boned chicken leg meat
½ tsp Szechuan pepper
400g green king prawns
1 tsp chopped or minced chilli
1 tsp chopped or minced garlic
1 tsp finely chopped or minced ginger
1 Tbsp chopped spring onions, white parts only
1 tsp coriander seeds
1 Tbsp coriander leaves
2 Tbsp peanut or light olive oil
1 tsp sesame oil
1 Tbsp thin strips of red sweet pepper
1 Tbsp thin strips of yellow sweet pepper
2 Tbsp coconut milk
Chopped spring onions, sweet pepper strips and coriander

METHOD
Cut chicken into bite-size pieces and sprinkle with Szechuan pepper. Set aside. Peel prawns. Put shells and heads in a saucepan and cover with water. Simmer gently for about 10 minutes to make a stock. Clean prawns and remove digestive tract by cutting along back and washing out any traces of black. Pat dry. Grind together chilli, garlic, ginger, spring onions and coriander seeds and leaves.

Put 1 Tbsp peanut or olive oil and the sesame oil in a wok or large frying pan and stir-fry chicken over high heat for 4-5 minutes. Remove and set aside. Stir-fry prawns for about 1 minute, adding more oil if necessary. Add sweet pepper and stir-fry for 30 seconds. Remove mixture. Add remaining oil and fry spice mixture for 30 seconds.

Strain prawn stock and pour 3-4 tablespoons into pan. Stir well. Remove pan from heat and add coconut milk. Add chicken, prawns and sweet pepper strips to pan and simmer over low heat for 5-6 minutes. Just before serving, stir in extra spring onions and sweet pepper strips and sprinkle with chopped coriander leaves.

Serving suggestion: Serve with rice.
Leftover potential: Keeps well and may be reheated or eaten cold.

Chicken Chardonnay

A variation on the *Coq au Vin* theme, it is best made using a good Australian Chardonnay. And of course a Chardonnay is the perfect wine companion. **Heart Foundation approved.**

Serves 4

INGREDIENTS
5 cloves garlic, peeled
1 Tbsp olive oil
1 Tbsp unsalted butter or low salt margarine
4 chicken Maryland pieces, skinned
2 Tbsp brandy (optional)
1 glass (250ml) Chardonnay wine
500ml low salt chicken or veal stock
1 tsp smooth Dijon style mustard
1-2 sprigs fresh tarragon or thyme

METHOD

Put garlic cloves, oil and butter or margarine into a large heavy-based saucepan over medium heat and cook until golden, taking care not to burn the garlic. Add chicken pieces and brown on both sides. Warm the brandy and flame the chicken. The brandy is optional but makes a difference to the final result. However a word of warning flaming should not be done in kitchens with low ceilings or by cooks with John Howard eyebrows! Once the flames have died down, remove chicken pieces and keep warm. Leave garlic in pan, add the wine, stock, mustard and tarragon or thyme. Stir well and cook for 5-10 minutes or until reduced by half, and the liquor has a syrupy consistency. Return chicken to the pan, spoon over liquor, cover tightly and simmer very, very slowly for 40 minutes.

Serving suggestion: When the chicken is cooked, serve on freshly cooked pasta. The sauce may be reduced over high heat if a thicker consistency is required.

Leftover potential: Keeps well for two or three days in the refrigerator.

Lemon Chicken

The lemon is a wonderful fruit and we should make more use of it in cooking, for both its juice and its rind. This recipe combines chicken and lemon in a simply prepared dish with a taste of the orient. I use thigh pieces - being on the bone, they don't dry out, so they are the best parts to have in a dish which is simmered.
Serves 4

Ingredients
1 kg lean skinless chicken pieces.
2 tspn finely chopped ginger
1 Tbsp reduced salt soy sauce
1 glass dry sherry
1 tspn sesame oil
Juice and grated rind of 1 large or 2 small lemon(s)
2 Tbsp honey
1 tspn olive oil
Spring onions (to garnish)
Lemon slices (to garnish)

Marinate the skinned chicken pieces in the soy sauce and the sesame oil for anything between an hour and a day. Make up a sauce using the grated lemon rind, lemon uice, the honey and the sherry, mix well. Drain the chicken, reserving the marinade. Pat the pieces dry with a kitchen towel and brown them in olive oil along with the ginger. When browned, pour in lemon and honey mixture and marinade, cover and let simmer for about 40 minutes. As always when simmering, just a very low heat, (bloopbloop sounds). When the dish is cooked you'll find that the sauce is not a thick one, but that's perfectly alright. Gone are the days when we have to thicken all sauces with flour. But you can remove the chicken and reduce the sauce to make it thicker if you wish. Garnish with chopped spring onions and some slices of lemon and serve with plain rice.

Meats

Once upon a time, actually about two years ago, meat meant red flesh. While beef and lamb are regarded as red meat, pork is being marketed in Australia as "the other white meat". In response to the increasing health awareness of today's consumers, producers are responding with leaner cuts. Recipes are also being tailored in recognition of the need to reduce the fat intake of our daily diet. When selecting meat it has always been my view that it pays to develop a rapport with a good butcher, preferably one who knows and cares about cooking as well as about the meat he or she is selling. You can leave it to her or him to select the best cut.

Fresh meat should have a clear pink or red colour without signs of grey or yellow. Meat should be stored loose-wrapped in the coldest part of the refrigerator . Minced meat and offal should be cooked the day it is bought. Large cuts may be kept for three or four days. Frozen meat will usually keep for up to six months in the freezer. The flavour of meat can be enhanced by marinating in a mixture of light oil and wine or lemon juice along with the herbs and spices of your choice. During the marinating process, juice is released from the meat so the marinade may be incorporated in the cooking. Veal should only be marinated for a couple of hours at most while other meats may be marinated overnight.

When cooking leaner cuts of meat the challenge is not to overcook them. With today's high standards of production, all meats may be safely cooked on the rare side — even pork.

Remember, if it's "well-done" it's over-done and that's not well done at all!

Pork And Orange Roll

Butcher Graham Jenkins of the Queen Victoria Market gave me this recipe. It is a speciality from his own kitchen. It is stuffed and roasted new-fashioned pork. **Heart Foundation approved.**

Serves 4 to 6

INGREDIENTS

A loin of pork (have your butcher trim off the fat and bone it)
2 tspn mixed dried herbs
Grated rind of 1 orange
1 tspn balsamic vinegar
1 onion, finely chopped
2 cloves garlic, crushed
Pinch of pepper
Breadcrumbs

With a very sharp, pointed knife, cut a pocket in the pork. Mix herbs, orange rind, vinegar, onion, pepper and garlic. Add breadcrumbs until it just holds a ball shape if you scoop it up in your hands. Stuff into the pocket. Close each end of pork with a satay stick. Bake at 160°C for about 25 minutes per kilogram. Test by inserting a satay stick or sharp knife in the meat. Juices should be clear. Serve with boiled potatoes and steamed green vegetables.

Orange Glazed Christmas Ham

Christmas is coming, the geese are getting lean. It's true. Gone are the days when we need to fatten our livestock for Christmas. When Christmas comes why not celebrate with a magnificent orange-glazed ham. Most hams are sold already cooked, cured and smoked. But by glazing our ham we can further enhance its flavour, reduce its fat content and make it look so attractive that you may find it difficult to spoil it by carving. **Heart Foundation approved.**

Serves everyone at Christmas (and then some!)

INGREDIENTS
A cooked ham on the bone
2 or 3 fresh oranges
20 or 30 cloves (yes, really)
1 cup honey
Orange liqueur
(Grand Marnier, Cointreau, or Curacao)

METHOD
Put the ham skin side up on a rack in a baking pan and remove the rind. This can easily be done by making an incision around the rind at the pointy end with a sharp knife, leaving just enough rind to use later as a handle. Using the knife, cut just under the rind at the blunt end of the ham. Then, by putting your fingers under the rind ease it away right back to the pointy end.

The fat can now be pared away with the knife taking care not to cut into the meat itself. Once that is done cut orange slices about 3 mm thick from the middle of the fruit, reserving the ends to squeeze for juice.

Smear 1 Tbsp of honey over the meat. I like to use an Australian wildflower or Tasmanian leatherwood honey. One by one, place the orange slices over the honeyed ham and fix them in position by gently forcing the cloves through them into the ham, about 5 to each slice.

As well as providing flavour and a delightful appearance, the cloves will stop the slices from slithering down the ham once the honey starts to melt in the oven. Once covered, the surface can be brushed with the remaining honey mixed with the orange juice squeezed from the reserved orange ends. Take care not to brush too hard in case you dislodge the orange slices. Now splash over a little orange liqueur. The alcohol will of course be cooked off. Sprinkle with raw or brown sugar and place in a moderate oven (about 180°C) for 1 hour.

Baste every 15 minutes with the honey and orange mixture which has dropped into the pan. When the ham is removed from the oven do a final basting and allow to cool before carving.

An easy way to carve is to hold the pointy end, cut out a wedge, then carve slices downward, finally removing them by cutting across the top of the bone. Now that you've spoilt your work of culinary art by carving it, serve it with hot or cold vegetables.

Pork and Apple Pie

An easy to prepare pie which works equally well hot or cold my preference is to serve it straight from the oven.

Serves 4

INGREDIENTS
Filling
500g minced pork

100g mushrooms, sliced
1 small onion, finely chopped
2 cloves garlic, finely chopped
1 large apple, finely chopped, peel included
1 large egg
½ tsp grated nutmeg
1 tsp grated lemon rind
50g pistachios (or other nuts of your choice)
Salt and pepper to taste
Breadcrumbs (preferably made with yesterday's bread)

To assemble
Puff pastry sheet
2 or 3 rashers bacon, rind removed
Slices of apple
1 egg yolk mixed with 1 Tbsp milk to glaze

METHOD
Mix together all filling ingredients, except breadcrumbs. Slowly mix in breadcrumbs to make a firm mixture. This usually requires 2-3 tablespoons of breadcrumbs. Cover a baking tray with baking paper then top with a large sheet of puff pastry. Put down a layer of bacon rashers. Top with a layer of apple slices then place filling mixture in the centre. Fold up sides and ends of pastry, joining at the top. Pinch pastry edges together to seal well. Brush top of pie with the egg and milk mixture. Bake at 190°C for 45 minutes or until pastry is golden and filling cooked.
Serving suggestion. The perfect accompaniment is Apple and Orange Sauce.
Leftover potential: Keeps two or three days in the refrigerator.

Apple and Orange Sauce

The perfect sauce to accompany patés and meat dishes such as the Pork and Apple Pie. **Heart Foundation approved.**

Serves 6

INGREDIENTS
3 medium apples, peeled and finely chopped
250ml low-salt chicken stock
250ml orange juice
2 tsp sugar
2 tsp Dijon-style mustard
2 cloves

METHOD
Put all ingredients in a heavy-based saucepan and cook over medium heat, stirring from time to time, until a thick chutney like sauce is made.

Leftover potential: Keeps well for two or three days in the refrigerator.

Herbed Lamb Balls

Greek-style meat balls made with herbs, spices and just a little Parmesan cheese.

Serves 6

INGREDIENTS
500g minced lean lamb
2 Tbsp finely chopped onion
2 eggs
1 Tbsp finely chopped oregano
2 tsp finely chopped rosemary
1 Tbsp grated Parmesan cheese
2 tsp ground cumin
½ tsp white pepper
Breadcrumbs (preferably made with day old bread)
Seasoned flour to coat balls
Oil for frying

METHOD
Mix together all ingredients, except the breadcrumbs. Slowly mix in breadcrumbs until you have a firm mixture. You'll probably need about 2 Tbsp of breadcrumbs. Shape mixture into balls about 3cm in diameter and roll lightly in seasoned flour. Either deep-fry or shallow-fry lamb balls in oil for 4-5 minutes. To check cooking time, try one once it's brown all over.

Serving suggestion: Delicious on their own as a snack or served with Lemony Mixed Vegetables
Leftover potential: Keeps for up to two days in the refrigerator.

Apricot and Herb Stuffed Loin of Pork

Lean pork is roasted with a filling of canned apricots seasoned with bacon, fresh herbs and spices, and glazed with a mixture of honey and soya sauce. Ask the butcher to remove the skin and make a pocket in the loin for stuffing. **Heart Foundation approved.**

Serves 8

INGREDIENTS

200g Australian canned apricots, drained and finely chopped
1 Tbsp chopped fresh thyme (or 1 tsp dried)
1 tsp mixed spice
1 tsp grated lemon rind
100g macadamia nuts, finely chopped
½ tsp white pepper
2 rashers bacon, fat and rind removed, chopped
1 medium onion, finely chopped
2 Tbsp strong chicken stock
1 egg
1 Tbsp brandy (optional)
Breadcrumbs
1½ kg boned loin of pork, skin and fat removed

Glaze
2 Tbsp honey mixed with 1 Tbsp reduced salt soya sauce

METHOD

To make stuffing, mix together apricots, thyme, mixed spice, lemon rind, nuts, pepper and bacon. Stir in onion. Stir in stock, egg and brandy (if using). Mix in enough breadcrumbs to make a stuffing with a firm consistency. Fill pocket in loin with stuffing take care note to overfill. Tie meat into a neat shape with butcher's (or other cotton). Brush pork with glaze. Roast at 180°C for 1½ hours, brushing with glaze every 15 minutes. Take care not to overcook.

Serving suggestion: Accompany with steamed green 1 vegetables of your choice.
Leftover potential: Excellent reheated or served cold.
Hint: Bake leftover stuffing mixture in a separate oiled baking dish for 15 minutes and serve with the pork.

Lamb Kebabs with Tabbouleh

Spiced up lamb cooked on skewers served with the classic Middle Eastern bulgar wheat salad. I buy the lightly cooked, dried and ground bulgar wheat for the salad, available from health food shops and delicatessens. **Heart Foundation approved**.

Serves 4

INGREDIENTS
750g lean fillet or leg lamb, trimmed of fat
1 onion, finely chopped
1 Tbsp chopped fresh rosemary (or 1 tsp dried)
2 Tbsp extra virgin olive oil
2 Tbsp lemon juice
Grated rind of lemon (optional)
1 Tbsp natural yoghurt
½ tsp paprika
1 tsp ground cumin
1 or 2 cloves garlic, finely chopped
Mixed vegetables of choice (courgette slices, cherry tomatoes, baby squash)

For Tabbouleh Salad

1 cup prepared bulgar wheat, soaked for 10 minutes in water
1 cup finely chopped parsley
½ cup finely chopped mint
2 Tbsp finely chopped tomato flesh
1 small Spanish onion, finely chopped
2 Tbsp finely chopped, peeled cucumber
About 2 Tbsp lemon juice (adjust to taste)
2 Tbsp extra virgin olive oil

METHOD

Cut meat into 2.5cm cubes and place in a bowl. Add onion and rosemary and toss. In a small bowl mix together oil, lemon juice, lemon rind if using, yoghurt, paprika, cumin and garlic. Stir yoghurt mixture into lamb. Cover and refrigerate for at least 4 hours, or overnight. Meanwhile, make the salad. Drain the bulgar wheat and mix with the other ingredients. Chill until needed. Thread lamb pieces and vegetables alternately onto bamboo skewers soak skewers in water to prevent burning. Baste kebabs with marinade and grill or barbecue, taking care not to overcook the meat.

Serving suggestion: Serve Kebabs with Tabbouleh Salad, flat pitta bread and Hazelnut Cream Dressing.

Leftover potential: Poor.

Hazelnut Cream Dressing

A good dressing to accompany simply cooked meats, such as lamb kebabs. **Heart Foundation approved.**

INGREDIENTS
100g hazelnuts, roasted
1 slice yesterday's bread, crust removed

300ml veal or chicken stock
4 cloves garlic
1 Tbsp lemon juice
2 Tbsp olive oil

METHOD
In a mortar or food processor, grind hazelnuts. Add bread, stock, garlic and lemon juice. Mix well. Slowly add olive oil. If it is too sloppy, add more bread. If too firm, add more oil.

Leftover potential: Keeps for several days in the refrigerator, but allow to come back to room temperature before serving.

Lamb Shank and Tomato Ragu

A little meat goes along way in this rich pasta sauce. Ask your butcher to cut the shanks through the bone so they can be folded over. **Heart Foundation approved.**

Serve 6

INGREDIENTS
4 lamb shanks, cut through the bone and trimmed of all fat
4 sprigs parsley
4 sprigs rosemary
8 small cloves garlic, peeled
2 Tbsp extra virgin olive oil
250ml red wine
1 medium carrot, grated
1 stalk celery, finely chopped
1 leek, finely sliced
1 kg ripe tomatoes (or equivalent canned tomatoes)

500g pasta of your choice

METHOD

Fold over each lamb shank and tie up with butcher's (or other cotton) string. Insert a sprig of parsley and rosemary, and a couple of cloves of garlic into each crack. Brown shanks in olive oil in a large saucepan.

Reduce heat, remove shanks and deglaze pan with splash of red wine. Add carrot, celery and leek and simmer gently for 5 minutes. Peel tomatoes and slice flesh. Push the seedy tomato pulp through a sieve into the pan. Discard seeds. Return shanks to the pan, cover tightly and simmer gently for about 5 hours. To serve: Cook pasta in lots of boiling water. Remove meat from bones and discard herbs and string. Top pasta with lamb and smother with the rich tomato sauce.

Leftover potential: Keeps for two or three days in the refrigerator.

Sweet Pepper Pork

If your knives are blunt, cut sweet pepper strips from the inside out. **Heart Foundation approved.**

Serves 4

INGREDIENTS
400g lean pork fillets
2 tsp sesame oil
1 Tbsp canola or peanut oil
1 yellow sweet pepper, cut into thin strips
1 red sweet pepper, cut into thin strips
1 medium-sized leek, cut into thin rings
1 fresh or dried chilli, seeds removed, flesh chopped (or 2 tsp minced chilli)

❧

2 tsp lemon juice
1 strip lemon rind
1 tsp tomato paste
2 Tbsp chicken stock
1 Tbsp peanut butter
Roasted peanuts, for garnish
Chopped fresh coriander or basil leaves for garnish

METHOD

Thinly slice the pork and place in a bowl. Add the sesame oil and marinate for a few minutes, while preparing the rest of the ingredients. Have all other ingredients standing by because once you begin cooking, you shouldn't need to leave the stove. Put half the canola or peanut oil in a frying pan or wok over high heat and quickly stir-fry the pork, a few pieces at a time until they just change colour, then remove to a warm place. Stir-fry sweet pepper strips for about 1 minute, reserving some for garnish. Remove from pan. Stir-fry leek for about 1 minute, adding a little more oil if it starts to stick. Now, with the leek still in the pan, add chilli, lemon juice, lemon rind, tomato paste, stock and peanut butter. Mix well. Return pork and sweet peppers to pan, reduce heat and simmer for about 2 minutes to allow pork to finish cooking. Garnish with reserved strips of sweet pepper, peanuts and coriander and basil.

Serving suggestion: Serve on a bed of rice.

Leftover potential: May be eaten cold as an acceptable salad

Spicy Spare Ribs

Pork spare ribs are marinated in a mixture of honey, five spice, coriander, sherry, sesame oil, soya sauce, chilli and tomato ketchup (sic). Although the ½ kg per person I allow may seem like a lot, remember that much of the weight is bone. This heavenly concoction is best made the day before it's cooked to allow the ribs to acquire the spiciness which makes the dish such a success.

Serves 4

INGREDIENTS
2 kg pork spare ribs (or beef, see note below)
2 Tbsp oil
2 Tbsp chopped coriander leaves to serve
2 Tbsp chopped spring onions to serve

Marinade
2 Tbsp sherry
2 Tbsp honey
2 Tbsp light soya sauce
2 tsp sesame oil
300ml tomato ketchup
½ tsp five spice powder
1 tsp ground coriander seeds
½ tsp white pepper

METHOD
Marinade: Mix together all marinade ingredients (omit chilli if serving to small children who may not care for it). Toss ribs in the marinade, put in an airtight container and refrigerate for at least 4 hours, or preferably overnight. Before cooking, drain ribs well and reserve marinade.

Sear ribs, a few at a time, in oil in a wok or frying pan to brown, then transfer to a baking tray. Bake the ribs at 210°C for 25 minutes (or until cooked), or they may also be barbecued. Whichever way you choose to cook them, baste frequently with the marinade. To serve, toss with the coriander leaves and spring onions and eat with your fingers.

Leftover potential: No, eat immediately.

Hint: When buying spare ribs, make sure there is meat on the bones. Tell the butcher how you intend using the ribs and I'm sure he or she will oblige. Ask for them to be cut into individual ribs. My preference is for pork ribs, but you could use beef.

Moussaka

A *Consuming Passions* version of this Greek or it could be Turkish classic. It's a much lighter dish than the moussaka that's customarily served in restaurants. **Heart Foundation approved**.

Serves 4

INGREDIENTS
1 large aubergine, cut into 1cm thick slices
Salt
Olive oil
500g minced lamb (or you could use beef)
2 Tbsp finely chopped onion
200ml red wine
1 tsp allspice
1 large can tomatoes (about 800g)
1 Tbsp chicken or veal stock
1 tsp chilli sauce
4 cloves garlic, crushed
2 tsp chopped rosemary (or ½ tsp dried)

1 Tbsp butter or polyunsaturated margarine
3 Tbsp cornflour
500ml reduced fat milk
100g low-fat mozzarella cheese, grated
1 Tbsp parmesan cheese, grated
½ tsp grated nutmeg
Pepper to taste

METHOD

Sprinkle aubergine with salt and stand for 30 minutes to remove bitter juices. Wash, drain and dry on paper towels. Brush aubergine with olive oil. Put on baking trays and bake at 180°C for 20 minutes, or until softened. This technique means that less oil is absorbed than if using the more traditional method of frying the aubergine. Cook meat in a little olive oil until it changes colour. It doesn't need to be thoroughly cooked at this stage. Add onion, wine, allspice, tomatoes, stock, chilli sauce, garlic and rosemary. Crush the tomatoes and cook slowly until mixture reduces to a thick sauce about 40 minutes. Make a roux by melting the butter or margarine over medium heat, stir in cornflour and cook for 2-3 minutes but don't allow it to brown. Slowly stir in milk and simmer, stirring, until you have a smooth sauce. Stir in mozzarella and parmesan cheeses and nutmeg. Season to taste.

To assemble: Alternate layers of aubergine with the tomato sauce in a baking dish, starting with a little sauce. Finally top with the bechamel sauce. Bake at 190°C for 30-40 minutes or until top is nicely browned.

Leftover potential: Good.

Hint: Can be made in advance, up to the cooking stage, and refrigerated. Allow 15 minutes longer cooking time if it's going straight from the refrigerator to the oven.

Osso Bucco

Osso bucco is one of Italy's classic meat dishes. A beautiful blend of veal, vegetables and wine patiently simmered and usually served with the equally renowned Italian rice dish risotto, and garnished with a gremolata. Ask your butcher for an osso bucco cut. Allow about ½ kg per person since much of the weight is in the bone and marrow which add to the flavour.

Serves 4

Ingredients
2 kgs osso bucco (veal or baby beef)
Plain flour for dusting shanks
2 carrots, sliced
1 large onion, finely chopped
1 leek cut into thin rings
1 tin tomatoes
1 stick celery, finely chopped
3 or 4 cloves garlic, finely chopped
2 Tbsp extra virgin olive oil
2 strips lemon rind
1 glass white wine
2 Tbsp brandy (optional)
500ml chicken stock
Basil and/or oregano leaves
Blackpepper

Using a heavy cookingpot, gently simmer onion, leek, carrot, celery and garlic in half the olive oil until onion has softened. Dust shanks with flour. Shake to remove excess. Remove vegetables from the pot. In the remaining oil, quickly brown veal shanks, a few at a time. If you opt to use the brandy — and I sincerely hope you do as it improves the flavour and is lot of fun — now is the time to flambe the meat. Put all shanks in pot and turn up heat. Warm brandy, strike a match. Pour brandy over shanks and touch flame to the vapours. Be careful of eyebrows and low flying aircraft! If there wasn't enough heat to flame it, it doesn't matter, the brandy flavours will infuse into the meat and the alcohol evaporate. Pack the shanks in a casserole dish as tightly as you can to stop them falling apart as they cook. Put vegetables and lemon rind into casserole dish. Add wine, stock and tinned tomatoes which have been broken up. Add a few basil and/or oregano leaves and a little black pepper.

Cover with tight fitting lid or foil and put in oven at 160°C for 2½ hours.

Gremolata

Combine grated rind of 1 lemon,
2 cloves of finely chopped garlic and 2 Tbsp chopped parsley
Serve with rice, steamed broccoli and a sprinkling of the gremolata

Moroccan Beef

A tantalising combination of traditional Moroccan spices and 'beefed up' with prunes and roasted almonds. Heart Foundation approved

Serves 6 to 8

Ingredients
1.25-1.4 kg beef cut in 4cm cubes
2 large Spanish onions, peeled and coarsely grated.
1 Tbsp olive oil
½ tspn each of freshly ground black pepper and powdered saffron

1 Tbsp powdered cinnamon
¼ tspn powdered ginger
450g dried prunes
4 Tbsp sugar
1 strip of lemon peel
2-3 short cinnamon sticks
225 g roasted almonds
Sprigs of fresh mint

Mix the meat cubes in a large bowl along with the onions, olive oil, black pepper and spices. Mix well, by rubbing the spices into each piece of meat with your fingers. Transfer the prepared meat to a thick-bottomed flameproof casserole and just ad enough water to cover the meat. Cover and cook over a medium heat until meat is tender, about 45-60 minutes. While this is cooking, prepare the prune sauce: Remove a cup of juice from the casserole, place in a small saucepan and remove any fat. Add half the sugar, the lemon peel and cinnamon sticks. Cook prunes in this mixture for 20 minutes or until they are soft and swollen. Transfer meat to serving dish and garnish with prunes and their sauce. Reduce remaining sauce in casserole to half its original volume over a high heat, then pour over meat and prunes. Sprinkle with roasted almonds, and garnish with sprigs of fresh mint. Serve on the spot with brown rice and steamed baby corgette, squash and carrots.

Beef Syrah

A cold weather treat named after the wine used to prepare the sauce which uses the Syrah grape and could be Shiraz or Hermitage. The meat benefits from being prepared the day before use. **Heart Foundation approved.**

Serves 4

INGREDIENTS
750g lean braising steak or other stewing beef
3 medium carrots
3 medium onions
5 cloves garlic, peeled
375 ml (half bottle) red wine
1 Tbsp olive oil
Sprig or two fresh thyme (or 1 tsp dried)
2 bay leaves
12 black olives, stoned
2 Tbsp strong beef or chicken stock
Pepper to taste

METHOD
Remove surplus fat from beef and cut into 2.5cm cubes. Chop carrots into similar sized pieces. Peel and quarter the onions. Place meat, carrots, onions, garlic and red wine in a non-reactive container and marinate for 4 hours, or overnight. Drain meat and vegetables, reserving the wine and vegetables. Pat meat cubes dry on paper towels. Brown meat, a few pieces at a time, in the olive oil over high heat in a frying pan. Set aside. Add reserved wine and vegetables, thyme, bay leaves, olives, stock and pepper to pan. Mix well, then add the meat. Half cover the pan and simmer very gently for at least 2 hours.

Serving suggestion: I like to serve it with creamy polenta and Chinese bok choy and the remaining wine.

Lamburger

A real Aussie burger. These are simple to prepare and an alternative to the humdrum beef versions found in the ubiquitous 'take-aways'.

Makes 8 burgers

Ingredients
1 kg minced lean lamb
1 tspn Tabasco or chilli sauce
2 cloves garlic, crushed
1 egg
150 g cooked rice
1 tspn curry powder
2 tspn cumin
2 tspn Dijon mustard
½ tspn pepper

Method
Mix all ingredients together and leave to stand for at least ½ hour to allow the flavours to develop in the meat. On a floured board, roll into burger shapes about 2cm thick. Grill for about 5 minutes on each side. They taste great served on a slice of homemade bread fresh, from the oven, with Basilled Tomatoes (see below) and a big green salad.

Basilled Tomatoes

A good salad to be served alongside a green salad or with hot or cold meat dishes

Serves 4 - 6

Ingredients
500 g tomatoes
Handful fresh basil leaves
Black pepper
1 Tbsp wine vinegar
3 Tbsp extra virgin olive oil

Method
Slice or dice tomatoes, chop fresh basil leaves and sprinkle over tomatoes. Season with pepper. Drizzle wine vinegar and olive oil over the salad just before serving.

Eggs

"What a hopeless cook. She (or he) couldn't even boil an egg." How often have we heard it said, or said it? Yet, it's a myth that cooking eggs is easy. Eggs are such complex little packages with so many properties that it's hardly any wonder it takes some skill to deal with them. There are many myths surrounding eggs. Let's explode a few. First, which came first, the chicken or the egg? Some theological lore maintains the chicken came first, arguing that God first created the creatures, not their means of reproduction. The Hindus argued that the world began with a golden egg. Chinese scriptures hold that an egg dropped from Heaven and hatched out man. Science has shown us the egg got here first. The egg as an entity could have evolved about a billion years ago in primitive form. It's believed that the shell came later, around 250 million years ago when reptiles took to living on the land and their eggs needed protection. The chicken that we know, *Gallus domesticus*, is a relative newcomer, which arrived on the scene around 5,000 years ago in South-East Asia or India, where it was first domesticated. It could be said that the chicken is simply the egg's way of making new eggs. And as nutrition goes, the egg is streets ahead of the chicken. This power-packed food has all the essential amino acids necessary for body-building and health, all the vitamins, with the exception of vitamin C, and more than a dozen minerals, including magnesium, phosphorus and that vital element, iron. For maximum benefit from the iron, which is lacking in many of us, it's a good idea to consume the egg with a food that has vitamin C, such as orange juice or green leafy vegetables, as this assists the body's absorption of iron. There is no more versatile food than the egg. As well as being enjoyed for itself cooked in hundreds of ways, it also contributes to making cakes and puddings, custards, ice-creams, mayonnaise and a host of savoury hot sauces. As for the great cholesterol myth, recent research by the CSIRO has shown that two eggs per day in the diet of people with normal cholesterol levels produced no rise in the level of undesirable LDL cholesterol. And even at three eggs per day, the effect on blood cholesterol was the equivalent of consuming a 10 gram pat of butter.

Tips with eggs

When buying, check there are no cracked eggs, which could harbour bacteria.

The colour of the shell makes no difference to the flavour or the nutritional quality of the egg. Nor does the colour of the yolk.

Store in the refrigerator in the carton you buy them in. They keep much better than in the egg compartments of the refrigerator. They should be stored pointy end down.

Eggs should not be stored near odorous foods, such as cut onions or melon, as they tend to absorb the smells. The exception is if you want to make truffled eggs, which are produced by storing the eggs with some small pieces of this hugely expensive fungus. Eggs will keep for several weeks in the refrigerator.

To test the freshness of an egg, lay it in a bowl of water. If it stays on its side on the bottom of the bowl it is really fresh. If it stands up on its pointy end, it is still reasonably fresh. If it floats, it's an old egg. Eggs should be brought to room temperature before use, as this will better their performance. The whites behave quite differently to the yolks, whisking up into fabulous meringues, while the yolks have an impressive emulsifying quality.

The egg whites are a terrific catalyst for clarifying stocks. If a couple of whites are stirred into a batch of cold stock and the stock is heated, the egg white will cook and float to the surface, taking with

ક

it any cloudy particles. Once strained, the stock will be perfectly clear.

To boil an egg, don't. It should be simmered. My favourite way to guarantee a soft-boiled egg is to put the egg in cold water and apply heat. When the water just reaches boiling point, turn down the heat and simmer the egg for 2 minutes, or 2 minutes 15 seconds for a large egg. Remove and hold briefly under cold running water to prevent further cooking. (Allow a few extra seconds if the egg has come straight from the fridge). An egg cooked this way should not crack in the water. Another way of preventing cracking is to pierce the fat end of the egg with a pin. That's where the air pocket is located.

To prevent black rings forming on hard-boiled eggs, simmer for 10 minutes then crack shell and plunge the egg into cold water. Really fresh egg whites do not whisk as well as older whites. When whisking egg whites, make sure the container and whisk are spotlessly clean. Avoid whisking in plastic bowls. Mix in a little cream of tartar to help stiffen the whites. A pinch of salt or a teaspoon of lemon juice may also be used.

Dishes made using raw egg yolk (such as mayonnaise or mouse) should be kept in the refrigerator for only a couple of days.

Scrambled Eggs

Few foods can be as disappointing as poorly made scrambled eggs. Yet they are easy to scramble to perfection. Try this foolproof recipe, which is made extra-special with the addition of smoked salmon.

Serves 4

INGREDIENTS
50g unsalted butter
9 large eggs
Salt and pepper to taste
1 Tbsp finely chopped chives or fresh dill
100g smoked salmon, finely sliced (optional)

METHOD
Melt butter in heavy-based saucepan over very low heat. Beat eggs lightly and carefully pour into butter. Cook very slowly, stirring frequently. While still soft, remove from heat, season to taste and stir in half the chopped chives or dill. Serve immediately topped with smoked salmon (if using) and remaining chives or dill.
Hint: Adding salt at the end of cooking will help prevent the eggs going watery. If eggs start to overcook, remove from heat and stir in 1 tablespoon of cream or milk.

Fruit Desserts

Australians are a fortunate people. Nowhere else in the world is there such a wide range of foods from which to choose and this is especially true in the case of fruit. Previously a nation of predominantly apple, pear and stone fruit eaters, we now have ready access to the fruits from all types of terrain and climate.

Fruits are related to vegetables and many foods that we call vegetables are, botanically speaking, fruits. For example, the aubergine and the tomato. One of the main differences between vegetables and fruit is that carbohydrate exists as starch in vegetables whereas in fruit it exists as sugars.

Apart from the delightful range of tastes and appearances, fruit is a great food because it is a ready source of vitamins and dietary fibre. With the exception of the avocado, they are also low in fat. A further health benefit is the presence in fruit of a little sodium and a lot of potassium. When buying fruit look for unblemished skin. The fruit should feel heavy for its size. Over-ripe fruit will smell musty.

Fruit is best bought as required and eaten immediately. If it needs further ripening it will do so better in paper bags with a few air holes for ventilation. By putting a ripe banana or apple in with the unripe ones, the ripening process is accelerated.

Try to avoid storing fruits such as apples, pears and stone fruit with their skins touching toprevent bruising. Always wash fruit in cold water before use, and do not store after being washed since they may deteriorate.

Most fruits will discolour after cutting, a natural process that may be impeded by smearing with any citrus juice. The citric acid will also enhance the fruit's flavour.

The rind of an orange or lemon is also a terrific flavour booster for other foods and enhances many meat and poultry dishes.

Cooking fruit in a sugar solution also prevents discolouring. Dried fruits may often be substituted for fresh fruits in recipes but it's worth remembering that dried fruit has the same amount of sugar but in concentrated form.

Flambéed Strawberries

An exciting way of serving strawberries, it may also be applied to other soft fruits such as bananas, peaches and apricots.

Serves 6

Ingredients
½ kg strawberries
1 Tbsp butter or margarine
1 Tbsp caster sugar
4 Tbsp brandy, cognac or orange liqueur
Low fat yoghurt and chopped nuts for serving

Remove stalks from the strawberries, wash and drain. Melt margarine in a heavy frying pan.
Add sugar and mix well. Pour in 2 Tbsp of brandy. Cook for a few seconds. Toss in the strawberries and warm for 1 minute so they are coated with the mixture.
Turn up the heat, pour in the rest of the brandy which has been gently heated. Set alight.
When the flame goes out, put strawberries in individual bowls and pour the sauce over them.
Serve with side dishes of low fat yoghurt and chopped nuts.

Freya Povey's Orange Cake

This is one of the tangiest cakes I have ever had the pleasure to eat. It is one of the simplest to make and requires neither butter nor flour. **Heart Foundation approved**

Serves 10 or more

INGREDIENTS
2 large oranges
250g ground almonds
250g raw sugar
5 large eggs
1 tspn bicarbonate of soda
2 tspn orange liquor (optional)

METHOD
Cook whole oranges in water for 2 hours. Drain, and allow to cool. Chop them into large pieces and blend peel and pith included. Beat eggs and sugar until creamed. Add other ingredients. Line a 20 cm cake tin with baking paper. Pour in mixture and bake in 200°C oven for 80-90 minutes. Check to see if its done by inserting a skewer. If ready it should come out clean. Allow to cool and serve.

Pears in Dessert Wine Sauce

Impress your dinner guests with this ridiculously easy dessert combining canned pears with a warm white wine sauce, served with a contrastingly cold vanilla ice-cream and topped with a crunchy almond praline. I find the dish is best made with an Australian botrytis-affected Semillon or Riesling (a so-called sticky) wine, but any good fruity white wine will do. **Heart Foundation approved.**

Serves 4

INGREDIENTS
250ml orange juice
Juice and rind of 1 lemon
1 Tbsp sugar
250ml dessert wine
1 cinnamon stick
2 or 3 cloves
8 halves of canned Australian pears, drained and juice or syrup reserved
Low-fat vanilla ice-cream, to serve

For praline
75g unblanched almonds
75g caster sugar

METHOD
Put orange juice, lemon juice and rind, sugar, wine, cinnamon stick, cloves and reserved pear juice in a non-reactive saucepan and cook over medium heat for about 15 minutes, or until reduced to one-quarter of its original volume, and a delicious syrup has

formed. To make praline: Put almonds and sugar in a heavy-based saucepan and cook over low heat, stirring, until sugar melts. Continue cooking over low heat until syrup is golden. Pour mixture onto an oiled baking tray and allow to set. Place praline in food processor and process to crush. Alternately, you can place the praline between sheets of baking paper and crush with a rolling pin. To serve: Pour a puddle of syrup onto each serving plate. Place a dollop of ice cream in the centre and stand the pear halves on either side. Sprinkle with a little praline.

Leftover potential: Cooked pears will keep in refrigerator for two or three days. Praline keeps almost indefinitely in an airtight container.

Fruit Flamri

This is a terrific and simple recipe based on an old semolina pudding recipe. Semolina is simmered with dessert wine, then sweetened, mixed with stiffly beaten egg whites and steamed to perfection. **Heart Foundation approved.**

Serves 6

INGREDIENTS
250ml water
250ml dessert wine (preferably a
botrytis-affected Riesling or Semillon)
125g fine semolina
2 large egg yolks
2 Tbsp caster sugar
2 large egg whites

For the berry sauce

※

100g fresh or frozen raspberries or other berries of your choice
1 Tbsp icing sugar

METHOD
Put water and wine in a heavy based saucepan. Bring to the boil, then reduce heat and stirring constantly, sprinkle in semolina. Simmer over low heat for 10 minutes, stirring occasionally. You should have a smooth mixture. If it dries out add a little more water it doesn't matter if there are a few small lumps. Beat egg yolks with caster sugar until sugar dissolves and the mixture is smooth. Beat egg whites until stiff peaks form. Make sure that the mixing bowl and whisk are perfectly clean. Adding ½ tsp cream of tartar will assist the process. Transfer semolina to a mixing bowl. Stir in egg yolk mixture, then fold in beaten egg whites. Make sure they're not wildly mixed in. The mixture must remain aerated. Drop dollops of mixture into greased ramekins or cups, cover lightly with plastic wrap and steam for 20 minutes. Allow flamris to cool a little before turning onto serving plates. For berry sauce: Push berries through a fine sieve. Stir in sugar and strain again. If the berries taste too sweet, add a little lemon juice.
Serving suggestion: Serve warm or cold with the berry sauce and fruits of your choice.
Leftover potential: Keeps for two or three days in refrigerator.

❧

Peach and Pecan Pizza

An easy dessert which may be prepared using a commercial pizza base or freshly made bread dough. I usually make a fruit pizza after I have made up a batch of bread and it really is worth the effort of making your own dough! Canned Australian pears may be substituted for peaches if preferred. Although my recipe uses mascarpone, an Italian-style double-cream cheese or a soft cream cheese could be substituted. For a healthy alternative, the Heart Foundation suggest serving this delicious dessert with yoghurt or ricotta cheese. **Heart Foundation approved.**

Serves 6

INGREDIENTS
1 ready-made pizza base or 250g homemade pizza dough
250g mascarpone (or other soft cream cheese), yoghurt or ricotta cheese to serve
For pizza dough
1 x 7g sachet dried yeast
1 tsp sugar
500g plain flour
Water at approximately blood heat (37°C)
1 Tbsp oil

For Peach and Pecan Topping
825g can Australian peach slices
2 Tbsp tangy orange marmalade with peel
½ tsp ground cinnamon
1 Tbsp melted butter or polyunsaturated margarine
100g chopped pecan nuts
2 Tbsp raw sugar

METHOD

To make dough: In a large mixing bowl, mix yeast with sugar, 1 Tbsp flour and 1 Tbsp water. Stand for 15 minutes to activate yeast the mixture will become frothy. Add the bulk of the remaining flour, leaving 2 Tbsp for kneading. Slowly stir in water until a firm dough forms.

Cover bowl with damp a tea towel. Put bowl in a warm place and leave dough to prove for about 1 hour, or until it doubles in size. Knead dough for 5 minutes on floured surface. Add more flour if dough keeps absorbing it and your hands become sticky.

Divide dough into two portions and roll out one piece for the dessert pizza. The other piece may be used to make a savoury pizza, bread rolls or frozen for later use. Grease a pizza tray and put dough on tray, pressing it out to fill the tray. Push the dough up the edges of the tray so that the juices will remain on the pizza and not dribble off the edge, which can happen with purchased pizza bases. Bake at 220°C for 10 minutes to partially cook. This is not necessary if using a pre-cooked commercial pizza base. For topping: While dough is baking, drain peaches and reserve juice. In a saucepan, mix marmalade with peach juice and cinnamon and cook over high heat until reduced to a thick syrup. Smear pizza base with melted butter or margarine then with thickened syrup. Decorate with peaches and pecan nuts, and sprinkle with sugar. Bake for a further 10 minutes to caramelise top and complete the cooking of the base. Serve hot, straight from the oven, with a generous helping of mascarpone, cream cheese, yoghurt or ricotta cheese.

Leftover potential: Best eaten same day.

Panforte
(Strong Bread)

Although this is a traditional Italian Christmas confection from Tuscany, it is perfect for any special occasion. Because there is quite a lot of work involved, I always make two at a time. For a darker, chocolate-flavoured panforte I add cocoa.

INGREDIENTS
200g raw hazelnuts, skin on
200g blanched almonds
50g raw macadamia nuts
200g citrus peel
100g dried figs, chopped
100g dried apricots, chopped
175g plain flour
2 tsp ground cinnamon
½ tsp ground coriander
½ tsp ground cloves
½ tsp grated nutmeg
½ tsp white pepper
2 tsp ground ginger
2 Tbsp cocoa (optional)
500g sugar
250g honey
125g unsalted butter

METHOD
Roast hazelnuts at 200°C for 15 minutes. When hazelnuts are slightly cooled, wrap in a tea towel and rub off skins. (It doesn't matter if some skin remains). Toast almonds in a dry pan until browned. Roughly chop the hazelnuts and almonds. It doesn't

matter if some whole nuts remain. Roughly chop macadamia nuts. Mix nuts with peel, figs, apricots, flour, cinnamon, coriander, cloves, nutmeg, pepper, ginger and cocoa (if using). Grease two 28cm springform cake tins and line base and inner wall with non-stick baking paper. In a saucepan, preferably non-stick, put sugar, honey and butter. Heat, stirring constantly, to 118°C on a sugar thermometer. If not using a sugar thermometer, keep cooking until mixture is smooth, bubbling fiercely, just starting to change colour, and reaches the soft ball stage. Quickly stir sugar mixture into fruit mixture. Divide mixture between prepared tins. Press down with a wet spoon, dipping it into water every few seconds to stop sticking. The mixture need not be spread evenly as it will soften and spread during cooking. Bake at 160°C for 30 minutes. Allow to cool, then remove from tin. Remove baking paper from base. Sprinkle with icing sugar.

Keep quality: Will keep well in an airtight container (as long as your family and friends don't discover it!)

Hint: The soft ball stage is reached when a small amount of sugar mixture dropped into water will roll into a soft ball in your fingers.

Banana Bread

The perfect recipe for using up those over-ripe bananas.

INGREDIENTS
300g ripe bananas, mashed with 1 tsp lemon juice
180g sugar
180g self raising flour
2 eggs
50ml milk
50ml nut oil
100g grated pecan nuts
100g grated bitter chocolate

METHOD
Combine bananas, sugar and flour. Add eggs, milk and oil and continue mixing for 2 minutes. Stir in nuts and chocolate. Pour mixture into a greased bread tin and bake at 180°C for 45-50 minutes.

Leftover potential: Keeps for two or three days in the refrigerator.

Nightingales' Nests

An Australian version of a Turkish classic, *Bulbul Yuvasi*, it is a sort of curly nut strudel made with macadamia nuts. I find a thin rolling pin or a piece of 1 cm dowel — is best for making these nests. **Heart Foundation approved.**

Serves 8

INGREDIENTS
200g macadamia nuts, finely chopped
1 Tbsp caster sugar
¼ tsp ground cinnamon
Grated rind of lemon (optional)
Light oil such as peanut or canola for brushing pastry
8 sheets of filo pastry
50g pistachio nuts, finely chopped, to garnish
Lemon Sauce
250g caster sugar
350ml water
1 Tbspn lemon juice

METHOD
Mix macadamia nuts with 1 Tbsp caster sugar and cinnamon. Dampen a tea towel, shake off surplus water and put on work bench as a working surface for the pastry. Put pastry sheets on the tea towel (allowing 1 sheet per nest). Brush each sheet lightly with oil. Sprinkle about 1 Tbsp of the nut mixture evenly over the top sheet of pastry. Put the rolling pin on a corner of the pastry, wrap a little of the top sheet of pastry over the rolling pin and roll up the sheet of pastry with the nut mixture on it. When it's rolled up, slide

the roll off the rolling pin and curl it into a snail-like shape. Repeat the process until all the pastry and mixture is used. Put the pastries on an oiled baking tray. Bake at 180°C for 25-30 minutes or until browned. Check frequently as small nests may take less time to cook. While the nests are cooking, make the sauce. To make the sauce, dissolve sugar in water and boil for 15 minutes. Remove from heat, add lemon juice and spoon hot sauce over the cooked nests. When cool, sprinkle with pistachio nuts and serve.

Leftover potential: Best eaten the same day or the next day at the latest.

Nut Crunchie

A particularly good topping for desserts, which keeps very well. This quantity serves eight, but larger quantities could be made to have on permanent stand-by. Store in an airtight container. **Heart Foundation approved.**

Serves 8

INGREDIENTS
1 Tbsp macadamia kernels (unsalted)
1 Tbsp blanched almonds
1 Tbsp pistachio kernels
1 Tbsp caster sugar
½ tsp ground cinnamon

METHOD

Finely chop the nuts or grind in a food processor. Don't overgrind or you'll finish up with a paste! Stir in the sugar and cinnamon.

Leftover potential: Keeps indefinitely in an airtight container.

Almond Pudding

Based on a Turkish recipe, this dish is the perfect partner for Fruit Compote. **Heart Foundation approved.**
Serves 6

INGREDIENTS

200g almond meal
400ml reduced fat milk
1 tsp almond or vanilla essence (whichever you prefer)
2 large egg yolks
2 Tbsp caster sugar
1 Tbsp cornflour

METHOD
Put almond meal, milk and almond or vanilla essence in saucepan and simmer over low heat for 10 minutes. Put egg yolks and caster sugar in a bowl and beat until sugar dissolves. Stir in cornflour and mix well. Bring milk mixture to boiling point, then pour onto egg mixture, stirring constantly. Pour mixture into a buttered or oiled ovenproof dish. Stand dish in a baking dish with enough water to come halfway up the sides of the dish. Bake at 160°C for 35 minutes or until the top has browned slightly. Cool a little before serving or serve cold.

Leftover potential: Keeps for two or three days in the refrigerator.

❧

Fruit Compote

A terrific all-purpose compote which may be served hot or cold at any time of year. In summer I make this dish with nectarines, peaches and apricots, and in winter with apples and pears or quinces. The only constant is black currants, which can be found all year round in frozen form. It works particularly well with Almond Pudding and Nut Crunchie. **Heart Foundation approved.**

Serves 4

INGREDIENTS
150g blackcurrants (frozen are fine)
2 Tbsp caster sugar
1 Tbsp honey
2 lime leaves (or lemon leaves or a strip of lemon rind)
500g seasonal fruits, cut into pieces

METHOD
Put blackcurrants, sugar, honey and lime leaves in a saucepan and cook over low heat for 10 minutes. Add fruit and simmer until fruits have softened a little, but still retain their shape.
Leftover potential: Keeps for two or three days in the refrigerator.

Kate Lamont's Citrus Quinces

Kate Lamont is a chef/restaurateur who firmly believes the partnership of wine and food begins in the kitchen. At her restaurant in Western Australia's Swan Valley, she uses wines produced at her parents' winery in several of her dishes. Although this recipe calls for quinces, it could also be made using firm pears. **Heart Foundation approved.**

Serves 6

INGREDIENTS
1 cup sugar
375 ml sweet white wine
Seeds scraped from ½ vanilla pod
(or ½ tsp vanilla essence)
2 lime leaves or 1 lemon leaf (optional)
1 cinnamon stick
Grated rind and juice of:
1 sweet grapefruit
1 orange
1 lemon
1 lime
4 quinces

To serve
300ml natural yoghurt (thickened by straining through clean cotton or muslin for at least 4 hours)
1 Tbsp honey
6-7 mint leaves, finely chopped

METHOD
Put sugar, wine, vanilla seeds and pod or essence, lime or lemon leaves (if using), cinnamon, and citrus juices and rinds in a non reactive saucepan (such as stainless steel or glass) and bring to the

boil to make a poaching syrup. Peel quinces and cut into thick slices. Immediately put quinces into syrup to prevent discoloration. Poach quinces for at least 1 hour, or until they are tender. Meanwhile, mix thickened yoghurt with honey. Cool quinces, serve with yoghurt and garnish with mint.

Leftover potential: Keeps for two or three days in the refrigerator and may be served cold or heated.
Hint: Low-fat yoghurt can be used.

Ginger Delights

A recipe from Buderim, Australia's ginger capital. **Heart Foundation approved.**

Serves 4

INGREDIENTS
200g strawberries
500g peeled bananas
1 mango
2 Tbsp ginger preserved in syrup, drained reserving syrup for sauce

For marinade
4 Tbsp light ginger wine
2 Tbsp chopped fresh mint

For flambé
2 Tbsp ginger liqueur or brandy, warmed

For sauce
2 Tbsp chocolate topping
1 Tbsp creme de menthe

METHOD

Marinade: Combine ginger wine and mint in a bowl. Hull strawberries. Cut bananas into 3cm chunks. Add strawberries and bananas to marinade. Cut mango into 3cm cubes and add to marinade. Soak bamboo skewers in water for 20 minutes, to prevent burning during cooking. Thread banana, mango, ginger pieces and strawberries alternatively onto skewers. Grill for 2-3 minutes over the open flame of a barbecue, basting with marinade, then flame with liqueur or brandy. Serve with sauce and garnish with fresh mint. *To make sauce*: Mix together chocolate topping, creme de menthe and syrup from ginger.

Leftover potential: Best eaten immediately.

Tangy Fruit Soup

An ideal entrée or dessert, this Scandinavian inspired refreshing soup is made in moments and may be served hot or cold. The recipe, which uses a mixture of fresh and canned Australian fruits, also makes a healthy breakfast! **Heart Foundation approved.**

Serves 8

INGREDIENTS
425g can Australian apricots, drained
825g can Australian plums, drained
¼ tsp ground cinnamon
1 Tbsp honey
500ml orange juice
Juice and grated rind of 1 lemon
250g seedless grapes, halved
4 Tbsp natural yoghurt (or creme fraiche or sour cream)

METHOD

Remove stones from apricots and plums. Purée apricots and plums in a food processor or press through a sieve, reserving some for garnish. Do this in batches if necessary. Add cinnamon, honey, orange juice and lemon juice and rind and continue blending. Chill for at least 2 hours before serving. To serve: Stir in grapes and top a generous dollop of yoghurt. Garnish with reserved fruits.

Eating Out A Few Pointers

Eating out can be every bit the challenge that cooking at home can be. And everyone has a responsibility to allow a consumer to get value for money; restaurateurs, waiters, chefs, and you, the patron. This guide will smooth the passage to a good meal out. There's also a tongue-in-cheek guide to what's IN and what's NOT.

Book your table in advance if possible, and notify the restaurant of any changes in numbers of diners.

Always let the restaurant know if you can't keep your booking. It's not just bad mannered, it's grossly unfair to restaurateurs to just not bother turning up they may have turned other customers away.

Bill splitting. It's a sensitive issue. Try to let the restaurant know if you intend bill splitting. Restaurants will often allow bill splitting if they're given notice and they're not desperately busy.

If a dish is not to your satisfaction, say so immediately, don't plough through it and then complain later.

By all means, ask for a recommendation of a wine to go with the meal. Most restaurants will be happy to help and won't rip you off. But watch out if you're offered that special wine that's not on the wine list.

Make sure the bottle is opened at the table so you know what you're getting.

Allow someone on your table to try the wine. And don't forget you're looking for faults in the wine, so don't send it back just because it's not to your taste.

If taking wine to a licensed restaurant, check the cost of the corkage.

If taking wine to a Bring Your Own restaurant and you don't know what you're going to be eating, a Semillon/Sauvignon Blanc or Chardonnay will usually work with fish, seafood, chicken and pork and a Cabernet Sauvignon or Shiraz (Hermitage) will accompany red meats, game, cheeses and dishes made with tomatoes. Sparkling whites make good aperitifs and meal finishers.

Tipping. Ask any restaurateur and they'll tell you their waiters are adequately paid. Certainly compared with some countries, where waiters rely on tips to earn a living. But they work hard for the money they get and I believe good service deserves recognition with a tip, especially if the restaurant has been very busy, and they've done a good job. Give direct to the waiter or it may not find its way back to him or her.

Treat waiters with respect.

Always get someone to check the bill.

If asked by the restaurant whether the meal was enjoyed, tell the truth!

What's In and What's Not

In

Mediterranean cuisine especially Moroccan and Eastern Mediterranean

South-west American cuisine

Preserved lemons

Lentils

Freshly made pasta

Balsamic vinegar

Real mayonnaise (always)

Ciabatta (flat slipper-shaped Italian bread)

Real bread of any kind

Virgin olive oil — instead of butter — on tables for dipping bread

Kervella goat cheese
Flying fish roe (seriously!)
Pearl barley
Sticky date puddings (always will be)
Waiters with powers of observation
The word 'waiter'
Being able to order food and pay the bill at the table
Domestic mineral waters
Australian wines
Lamb

Out
Silver Service Dining
Sun-dried tomatoes
Alfalfa sprouts
Baby squash
Al Dente potatoes
Iceberg lettuces
Commercial mayonnaise
Imported mineral waters
Garnish you can't eat
Artificial flowers
White plastic furniture
Large laminated menus
Tiny tables and large designer plates
Napkins in dispensers
The word "waitperson" (whatever sex, they're all waiters!)
Surly, visually challenged waiters (who look but don't see)
Pestering, grovelling or chummy service
Having to pay the bill at the desk on the way out
Mobile phones
WACA-intensity lighting
Lighting so dim you can't see what you're eating
Inferior European wines

OVEN TEMPERATURES

	°C	°F	Gas Mark
Very Low	120	250	
Low	150	300	2
Mod. Low	160	325	3
Moderate	180	350	4
Mod. Hot	190	375	5
Hot	200	400	6
Very Hot	230	450	8

DRY INGREDIENTS

Metric	Imperial
15g	1½oz
30g	1oz
45g	1½oz
60g	2oz
75g	2½oz
100g	3½oz
125g	4oz
155g	5oz
185g	6oz
200g	6½oz
250g	8oz
300g	9½oz
350g	11oz
375g	12oz
400g	12½oz
425g	13½oz
440g	14oz
470g	15oz
500g	1lb (16oz)
750g	1lb 8oz
1kg (1000g)	2lb

CUP & SPOON

1 cup   250m $\frac{1}{8}$fl oz
½ cup 125m ¼fl oz
1/3 cup 80ml
¼ cup 60m ½fl oz
1 Tbsp 20ml
1 tspn 5ml
½ tspn 2.5ml
¼ tspn 1.25ml

LIQUIDS

Metric	Imperial
30ml	1fl oz
60ml	2fl oz
100ml	3 lt2fl oz
125ml	4fl oz(½ cup)
155ml	5fl oz
170ml	5½fl oz(2/3 cup)
200ml	6½fl oz
250ml	8fl oz (1 cup)
300ml	9½fl oz
375ml	12fl oz
410ml	13fl oz
470ml	15fl oz
500ml	16fl oz (2 cups)
600ml	1pt (20fl oz)
750ml	1pt5fl oz (3 cups)
1litre	1pt12fl oz (4 cups)